Progres
Love Jesus Too

A Response to Alisa Childers

(and the heresy hunters)

2 CUP
PRESS

Canada

Progressive Christians Love Jesus Too

Book cover by Darryl Frayne–steadydigital.ca

*This book is for every Christian
who ever asked a hard question
or expressed an honest doubt
only to be shamed into silence.
Don't be intimidated.
You are true Israel.*

Contents

Acknowledgements

This is the fourth book I have published under my own imprint, 2 Cup Press. In each case, my friend Darryl Frayne of steadydigital.ca has proven to be an invaluable resource in developing the covers and helping me troubleshoot the finer points of typesetting. I'd also like to thank Peter Enns for joining me in conversation on these topics: Pete, you represent the best of the progressive Christian conversation, even if you don't call yourself one!

Lastly, I'd like to tip my hat to my Lhasa Apso, Sonny. I've authored fourteen books (including three as a coauthor) and this is the first one that was written without Sonny curled up at my feet: he passed away on February 9, 2022 at the ripe old age of 18 (and a half). The following story tells you who Sonny was: on one occasion, I found the old boy completely still on the back lawn, tail gently wagging, head resting on his front paws, staring intently into the grass. He had found an injured sparrow and was exhibiting his trademark concern and protectiveness. Sonny was such a gentle spirit and while he is gone, his presence abides in these pages. Enjoy your time over the rainbow bridge, dear friend. Rest assured, we shall meet again in the new creation where sparrows are never injured, and beloved dogs never grow old.

Foreword

Definitely Not by Lee Strobel

Christian apologist Lee Strobel provided a glowing foreword to Alisa Childers' book *Another Gospel?* Given that fact, I was pretty sure he wouldn't agree to do a foreword for my book. So, I figured if I couldn't have a foreword *by* Strobel, I'd write one about his foreword for Childers' book instead. More specifically, I want to focus on one sentence in Strobel's foreword. He writes: "In Christianity, the anchor is sound biblical doctrine."[1] In making this statement, Strobel is very much on the same page as the book he is endorsing, and thus his maxim serves as something of a theme for the book itself: for Strobel and Childers, doctrine is the foundation of Christianity.

I could not disagree more. And lest you hastily conclude that means I don't *care* about doctrine, the matter is quite the opposite: I am a systematic theologian who has been teaching theology in seminaries and colleges for twenty years. The truth is that thinking about doctrine is my vocation and my passion. Indeed, that is precisely *why* I emphatically disagree with the claim that Christianity is anchored in doctrine: you don't honor something by completely misunderstanding its function and role in the Christian life. And making doctrine the foundation does that.

So let us be clear: the anchor for Christianity is not doctrine.

---

1 Lee Strobel, "Foreword," in Childers, *Another Gospel? A lifelong Christian Seeks Truth in Response to Progressive Christianity* (Tyndale, 2020), xiii.

It is Jesus Christ. He is the chief cornerstone (Psalm 118:22; Matthew 21:42), the Rock (1 Corinthians 10:4), the head of the Church (Ephesians 1:22), the Great High Priest (Hebrews 4:14), the Advocate (1 John 2:1), the Mediator (1 Timothy 2:5), the Good Shepherd (John 10:11), the Way, the Truth, and the Life (John 14:6), and so much more.

We have been crucified with Christ and baptized in him, and we now live in him as we await the resurrection (Romans 6:1-8). He reveals the Father to us (John 14:9) and reconciles us to the Father (2 Corinthians 5:19). And he sent the Spirit of Truth to lead us into truth (John 14:16-17; John 14:26) and dwell within us (1 Corinthians 3:16). To conclude, the anchor is Christ through whom we are drawn into the triune life of God (2 Peter 1:4).

You might be thinking, "Yes, but those are all *doctrines*, are they not?" Well sure, we *describe* the reality of God's saving actions in terms of doctrines, but confusing God's actions with our descriptions of them is equivalent to confusing a description of your spouse with your spouse. These are very different things: best not to confuse them.

Lest you still think I'm splitting hairs between doctrine and Christ, ask yourself: *what is the foundation of a family?* Is it the relationship *with* the family or the beliefs one holds *about* the family? A few years ago, my father was diagnosed with Alzheimer's Disease. I will never forget the afternoon not long after the terrible news when he looked at us with sad eyes and whispered: "I'm going to forget you." 'Yes," I replied, "but we will never forget you." If beliefs were the foundation of our family, Alzheimer's would have eroded my dad's place within it down to nothing. But the truth is that my father remained as much the husband of his wife and the father of his sons on the day he died as he ever was. The anchor for our family, and my father's central role within it, was not our beliefs about one another: rather, it was ever and always *relationship*. How much more is this true when we speak of the family of God?

If this error were Strobel's alone, it might not be worth mentioning. But as I said, Childers commits the same error. For example, consider the following passage in which she targets the emergent church, a movement that she takes to be a forerunner of progressive Christianity:

> Historically, Christians have viewed good works and acts of justice to be a *fruit* of their convictions. Believing the right things about God produces right actions. However, the emergent church flipped this on its head. Things like community, friendship, justice, and unity became the foundation upon which one's faith is built.[2]

Building a community on friendship, justice, and unity: sounds pretty good to me! Alas, Childers seems to think otherwise. What is more, her wording suggests that there was a Christian historical consensus for centuries to the contrary, one that insisted doctrine is the foundation. She also wants us to believe that this consensus was not seriously challenged until the emergent Christians of twenty years ago came along. This is simply an absurd claim. Christians throughout church history have held a diversity of views on such matters. To put it bluntly, Childers' claim that her own highly intellectualized view of Christianity is the consensus position of all church history is a bald attempt to quash dissenting voices by appeal to a *force majeure* of historical consensus that simply doesn't exist.

Consider this simple fact: over several centuries, *infant baptism has historically been the predominant form of the rite of initiation into the community of faith.* Theologians have offered various frameworks for understanding the rite including the concept that infants may have implicit (i.e. non-cognitive) faith or that the parents' faith may act as proxy for the absence of faith in the child. Regardless, the fact remains that most Christians throughout history have uncoupled the welcome into

---

2 Childers, *Another Gospel?* 73.

the Christian community from cognitive assent to doctrine.[3] If the rite of initiation into the community is not essentially connected to a person's assent to doctrines, how can one claim doctrinal assent is the foundation for all else (including the rite of initiation itself)?

What consequences might follow from Strobel and Childers' prioritization of the cognitive assent to doctrine over relationship? First, because Childers makes doctrine the anchor for Christianity itself, she is surprisingly quick to conclude that those who do not accept her conservative evangelical theology have a non-Christian foundation. For example, as we will see in chapter 8, Childers boldly insists that Christians who fail to accept her view of the atonement are *not even Christians*. Time and again, when Christians question her preferred understandings of doctrine, Childers concludes that they are heretics or they even belong to another religion: given that doctrine just is the anchor, there is little room for theological diversity in this fragile, rationalist notion of Christianity.

The matter is very different, however, when you believe that relationship precedes and is the foundation for doctrine. A healthy and deep relationship welcomes hard questions and deep discussions, and it is no different when the relationship is with the Father, in the Son, through the Spirit. In that famous story of national origin, Jacob wrestles with the Angel of the Lord through the night (Genesis 32:22-32). As a result, he is blessed with a new name: *Israel*, or *he who wrestles with God*. Within Hebrew culture, your name identifies who you are. And so it is that God's people are known as those who wrestle with God. And that wrestling requires the freedom that relationship provides to ask honest, hard questions. The very fact that we are willing and keen to ask hard questions is a *testament to* our devotion for the conversation is borne by the relationship.

---

3 In the book, Childers cites Norman Geisler's qualification that belief must be at least "implicit" but it is not at all clear what that means. We will discuss the significant difficulties with this view in chapter 10.

As we will see, the various people that Childers groups together as "progressive Christians" are a very diverse bunch with a range of doctrinal views, some of which I would agree with and others, not so much. But what they all share and what I heartily embrace is a recognition that doctrine is not the anchor of Christianity: Christ is. And the more we love God the more we are willing to wrestle boldly with him through the night.

So come, let us wrestle.

Introduction

to All That Comes After

This book is an extended rebuttal to the book *Another Gospel?* by Alisa Childers. For that reason, you might assume that it has a rather narrow scope and that you need to have read Childers' book or have an interest in her work in order to find this a worthwhile read. Neither of those assumptions is true. While Childers' work is in the foreground, one can view my critique as responding to leaps of logic and talking points that are common in contemporary evangelicalism. Given that conservative evangelicalism is a major cultural force in North America, packing suburban churches and producing a string of celebrity pastors, evangelists, and apologists, I believe this is a conversation with implications extending far beyond Alisa Childers.

We have already been introduced to some common features of this conservative evangelicalism in our "Foreword Definitely Not By Lee Strobel." (So, if you skipped the Foreword as some impatient readers are apt to do, please go back and read it: don't worry, I'll wait.) The difference between Childers (and Strobel) and the progressive Christians she attacks is captured in Strobel's errant notion that Christianity is anchored in doctrine. As I said in the Foreword, this is a mistaken notion: just as a family is anchored in relationship rather than the beliefs the family members hold about each other, so Christianity is anchored in Christ rather than our doctrines about Christ: get those things mixed up, and some pretty serious consequences can follow.

More about all that to come. But for now, here is a quick overview of the road ahead.

Chapter 1 introduces *Another Gospel?* while highlighting the key story that frames the book, namely that some years ago Childers participated in a course to rethink her faith which was led by a progressive Christian pastor. This course with its process of deconstruction so troubled and disturbed her that it launched a journey which culminated in her book-length take-down of progressive Christians. The irony, as we shall see, is that the course itself clearly had a *positive* if painful impact upon Childers, though she seems loathe to admit it.

Chapter 2 introduces the concept of the binary mindset which forces complex facts, situations, and persons into simple either/or oppositions. Those who react to the stress of deconstruction by retreating further into the binary mindset become even less able to process new information or adapt to changing and nuanced circumstances. And this predisposes the individual to fall into a heresy hunting mentality that defines oneself over-against perceived enemies of the faith locked in a spiritual battle of good versus evil.

For the remaining eight chapters, we will focus on rebutting specific false assumptions and assertions in *Another Gospel?* We will begin in chapter 3 by arguing that "Progressive Christianity is Not a New Religion." In the chapter, we will consider how Childers attempts to describe progressive Christianity as a distinct movement and indeed *another religion with another gospel.* In point of fact, that which is commonly called progressive Christianity is nothing more than a broad coalition of interests to promote open questioning and critical reflection. Further, as we will see, several of the people Childers cavalierly denounces as false Christians are, in fact, respected Christian thought leaders from a diverse array of backgrounds united in this interest in and commitment to wrestling with God in Christian community.

In chapter 4, "Humility About Knowledge is Not Relativism about Truth" we will respond to Childers' misguided accusations that progressive Christians reject objective truth in favor of a radical relativism. As we will see, her misdiagnosis is rooted in her inability to distinguish epistemic humility (that is, an awareness of our limitations in *knowing* truth) from relativism about truth. In short, these progressive Christian leaders are not rejecting the *existence* of objective truth but rather cautioning us about the extent of our *grasp* of it.

Next, we will turn in chapter 5 to the topic "Doubt is Not Separate from Disbelief." As we will see, Childers attempts to argue that unbelief and doubt are categorically different things with unbelief being borne by sinful rebellion while doubt, by contrast, is innocent as it arises in the context of faith. On the contrary, I will argue that this is an erroneous distinction: the truth is that doubt and unbelief together exist on a continuum of belief that extends between certainty that a proposition is true and certainty that it is false. Once we recognize that fact, we can see that we all exist on a *spectrum* of belief. And this, in turn, undermines Childers' insistence that all unbelief is borne of sinful rebellion.

In chapter 6, "Progressive Revelation is Not Error-Free," I will address Childers' understanding of progressive revelation. She insists that while progressive revelation exists, it is always error-free. I will argue against this claim and demonstrate by way of the concept of accommodation and several specific examples that God's progressive revelation to his people involves accommodation to some degree of error through time. And this, in turn, requires the Christian to consider seriously where error may be present in the process from the biblical authors, down through church history, and to our own age.

In chapter 7, "Biblical Inspiration Does Not Extend to Interpretations," we will explore the confusion that arises in Childers' understanding of inspiration and the role of the interpreter. I will point out that human readers are always fallible interpreters and thus we can recognize the authoritative inspiration of Scripture alongside the fallible and limited nature of our interpretations (and thus our grasp) of that inspiration. Alas, Childers fails to make this distinction and as a result, she is prone to collapse her *interpretation of the text* into the *inspired authority of the text*. Thus, she assumes that people who don't share her interpretation of the Bible are thereby rejecting the Bible. (Needless to say, it ain't necessarily so.)

In chapter 8, "The Atonement is Not Penal Substitution," we will turn to consider one of the most significant and overt confusions in *Another Gospel?* with Childers' failure to distinguish the Christian *doctrine* of atonement from the penal substitutionary *theory* of atonement. Based on this confusion, she assumes that anyone who rejects the theory of penal substitution thereby rejects the doctrine of atonement. This leads her to the brazen accusation that progressive Christians reject the Christian Gospel for "another gospel." Childers is profoundly misguided here: the orthodox Christian church has *never* required assent to one interpretation of atonement, and certainly not the penal substitutionary theory.

In chapter 9, "Final Judgment is Not Eternal Conscious Torment," we will consider yet another elementary confusion in the book as Childers conflates her eternal conscious torment theory of hell with the doctrine of hell as such. Based on this confusion, she assumes that anyone who rejects the eternal conscious torment theory thereby rejects the doctrine of hell. This is false, for there are two other major theories of posthumous judgment and hell in the Christian tradition: annihilationism and universalism. What is more, Childers falsely says that universalism (the idea that all creatures will eventually be reconciled to the Father through Christ) is heretical: it is not. I will conclude the chapter by noting some of the several reasons why other Christians have rejected eternal conscious torment beginning with the fact that this theory entails that God *tortures* people for eternity.

We will conclude our analysis in chapter 10, "Salvation is Not a List of Beliefs" by returning to where we started with Childers' mistaken notion that Christianity is anchored in Christian doctrine rather than Christ. At this point, we will focus on Childers' extraordinary claim that salvation requires assent to eight specific doctrines. I will argue against this view by seeking to illustrate some of the significant problems that arise when one attempts to reify any specific set of doctrines as being necessary for salvation.

And with that, we end where we began, by noting that relationship precedes doctrines and provides the anchor for them rather than vice versa. And it is God who wills it so.

1

Alisa Childers

and the Progressive Pastor

Alisa Childers is the daughter of Chuck Girard, a Christian rock and roll pioneer famous for his early 1970s folk rock group Love Song. Back in the 1980s, I remember listening to Love Song on record alongside other fossils from that cultural epoch like Larry Norman and Resurrection Band. (Gee, now I really sound old.) Growing up with an early Christian folk rock legend as your dad, Childers was "The one you would never worry about. The one you just knew would be fine."[4] Once she had become an adult, Childers herself enjoyed some popularity in the music business in the early 2000s with the Christian pop group zoEgirl. To sum up, when it comes to conservative evangelical credentials, you could hardly do better if your last name was "Graham."

Alisa married Mike Childers, the drummer from zoEgirl, and together they began to raise a family. At this time, the young couple started attending a church with a dynamic young pastor. Not long after their arrival, the pastor invited Childers

---

4 Childers, *Another Gospel?* 5.

to join a select group of congregants with the idea that together they would embark on a journey of critical and honest theological reflection exploring Christian faith. However, things didn't go as Childers (or the pastor) had planned. Far from growing in her understanding of Christianity, Childers soon suffered a "faith crisis" as she was left to grapple week after week with questions she had never considered and to which she did not have answers.

Even worse, it wasn't long before Childers was beginning to suspect that this pastor and the other students didn't really *want* to get answers. She eventually concluded that their real goal was much more sinister: the subversion of the orthodox Christian faith given once for all unto the saints. And so, after just a few months, Childers decided to withdraw. She recalls, "The class lasted four years. I lasted four months."[5]

Although that spiritual crisis unfolded more than a decade ago, Childers still seems to be angry about the whole experience. In fact, time seems to have only sharpened her analysis. Childers now views the class as a sham and the pastor's role as a fundamental betrayal. With some bitterness she likens her experience to a hapless young Christian student having their Christian faith dismantled by a malicious skeptical university professor. For example, think of the stereotyped evil atheist philosophy prof played by Kevin Sorbo in the movie *God's Not Dead*. The guy acts as if his life's mission is to destroy the faith of unsuspecting Christian students. Folk like that professor are not people of goodwill honestly seeking truth; rather, they are deceivers who desire to lead God's people into lies. As Childers puts it, her faith was "rocked by a pastor who had won my trust, respect, and loyalty."[6] In essence, she was tricked with the promise that she would grow into her faith when the real goal was to undercut her beliefs and foment the crisis that shook her to her foundations: the ultimate bait-and-switch.

5 Childers, *Another Gospel?* 6.

6 Childers, *Another Gospel?* 6.

Childers definitely offers a stark analysis of her experience, one told with a one-dimensional cast of heroes and villains. This black-and-white narration sets the tone for the book with the progressive pastor providing the template for many other malicious and deceptive fake Christians, people that Childers insists mask their true identities and motives behind the inviting moniker of progressive Christianity. In this chapter and the next, I want to seek a further understanding for why Childers automatically retreats to such a stark and uncharitable account. Why assume the pastor was a malevolent deceiver? Why assume the fellow students didn't really care about the truth? Why assume progressive Christians are opposed to Christianity?

In order to answer these questions, we will begin by looking at the revealing way that Childers describes her own Christian upbringing and how that set her up to experience a crisis of faith. We will then consider how this predisposes her to be defensive, to interpret the pastor's intentions as malicious, and to take his statements in a consistently negative manner when charitable interpretations are readily available. I will conclude with some words on education and the process of deconstruction and how that can lead to blowback from those who are unable to process the experience.

A Spotlight on the Past

As we read through the book, it becomes clear that there were some significant gaps in Childers' Christian upbringing because she tells us as much. While Childers insists that she didn't grow up with a "blind faith," she admits that her faith was "intellectually weak and untested."[7] For example, she states that while she had high confidence in the Bible prior to taking the class, she didn't know why: "Before starting the class, I was absolutely and wholeheartedly convinced that the Bible was

---

7 Childers, *Another Gospel?* 5.

the Word of God—inspired, inerrant, and infallible. But other than having been taught that, *I had no idea why I believed it.*[8] As she candidly admits, "I realized that I had based my whole life on a book, and I had no intellectual reason to explain why."[9]

Not only was the faith with which Childers was raised intellectually weak and untested, but in some respects, I think it can be described as spiritually abusive. Strong words, I know, but consider what she says regarding the way she was taught to think about hell and eternity. In her chapter on hell, she begins by describing how her second-grade Sunday school teacher addressed the topic. The teacher told them:

> Everyone in this class is at least seven years old. Did you know that *seven* is the age of accountability? That means that if by seven years old you haven't received Jesus as your personal Lord and Savior, you will be on fire in hell forever while worms slowly eat your flesh for all eternity.[10]

Imagine being told as a little kid that God would make you burn in fire forever with worms gnawing through your flesh! I was raised in a conservative evangelical / borderline fundamentalist church tradition, so I heard more than my share about hell and a lot of it was quite awful. But even so, I don't recall ever being taught anything nearly this cruel and abusive: what an absolutely appalling thing to say to a child! To terrify small children in this manner is spiritual abuse, period.

Hell is bad enough, but to make matters worse, the trauma extended to Childers' understanding of heaven as well. She was apparently raised as a dispensationalist. A unique feature of that modern theological tradition (it was developed in the 1860s) is a doctrine called the secret rapture according to which Jesus will come back not once but *twice*: the first return

8 Childers, *Another Gospel?* 119.

9 Childers, *Another Gospel?* 120.

10 Childers, *Another Gospel?* 177.

will be a secret one in which he whisks his followers out of the world followed by a second public return of fire and judgment. Childers recalls that as a child she was taught this secret rapture. However, far from being a comfort that the chosen few will be whisked to safety before the bombing starts, it only added to the stress and misery:

> This was supposed to be "good news," but for an eight-year-old already living in almost constant existential crisis, the idea of Jesus unexpectedly beaming his followers up to heaven sounded just about as terrifying as the hordes of insatiable zombie worms that were waiting to feast on my face.[11]

I was raised in a denomination with dispensational theology (the Pentecostal Assemblies of Canada) and I experienced some of the existential angst created by the rapture doctrine, so I can understand what Childers is saying here from the inside. When you're a kid, stories like the parable of the wise and foolish virgins can haunt you (Matthew 25:1-13). The lesson is that if you're not following Jesus just right every day, then when he secretly returns you may miss him and be left behind to face the cataclysms that dispensationalists confidently predicted would soon befall the earth based on their reading of Revelation and the newspaper. It was the ultimate expression of the fear of missing out.

For example, I remember once as a child waking up from a nap. I called out for my mom and dad, but nobody answered. After a quick run through the house, I couldn't find anybody. For fifteen terrifying minutes, I was convinced that my family had been raptured to heaven and I'd been left behind! I still recall the overwhelming sense of relief when I discovered I hadn't been left behind after all: everyone had simply migrated to the backyard. So even if I can't quite resonate with Childers'

---

11 Childers, *Another Gospel?* 178.

statement that "fear and panic became my new normal,"[12] I can certainly understand how the constant stress and vigilance created by the secret rapture doctrine could be a generous amplifier of pre-teen angst. And when that stressor was overlaid on the ever-present stress about hell, the impact could be some significant emotional and spiritual damage.

Thus, when Childers entered the classroom to begin the journey with the progressive pastor and fellow students, she brought with her an intellectually shallow understanding of her faith and some not insignificant emotional and spiritual baggage created by some disturbing doctrines combined with questionable Sunday school pedagogy. In a situation like this, you can anticipate that the upheaval for a student confronting the vast theological gaps and spiritual abuse of their past could be traumatic. And it clearly was. As Childers looks back on the four months that she spent in the progressive pastor's group she says it was "like Jacob wrestling with God" and that it left her "walking with a limp." She adds, "The class that would permanently embed the voice of a skeptic into my mind—that has to this day affected my ability to read the Bible without inner conflict."[13]

To be honest, this doesn't sound to me like a bad result. In the case of Jacob, walking with a limp was a badge of honor, a sign that he had *persevered* and *received a blessing*. By her own admission, Childers came to the class with an "intellectually weak and untested" faith and, even after just four months, she left with a skeptical voice that would challenge her previously naive thinking going forward. Granted, she says that voice would leave her with "inner conflict," but why think that conflict is necessarily a *bad* thing? On the contrary, this sounds to me like a good description of intellectual and spiritual *growth*. Here we have an individual who was raised with an intellectually weak and untested faith, but after just

---

12 Childers, *Another Gospel?* 178-9.

13 Childers, *Another Gospel?* 20-1.

fourth months of wrestling with Christianity in community like Jacob wrestled with the angel, the individual now walks with a limp accompanied by a new voice of critical, reflective doubt. I'd say that's a *good* result!

Unfortunately, Childers does not see things that way. Rather, she seems to view the class in wholly negative terms, a betrayal by a wolf dressed up as a shepherd, one who was "hell-bent" (her words) on undermining her Christian faith altogether. What explains this response?

Turning Friends into Enemies

We will devote much of the next chapter to seeking a fuller understanding of *why* Childers defaults so readily to narrating her experience in the class in terms of a black and white clash between good and evil, heroes and villains. For now, however, I want to begin by considering some of the specific ways that she begins to make the pastor a villain in the story, one seeking to undermine and destroy the faith of his benighted, trusting flock.

While that may sound dramatic, that really is how Childers appears to view things. This pastor and others like him are tools of the devil aiming to destroy the church. As she puts it, "progressive Christianity is a movement not satisfied to sit in the margins. It is directly aimed at infiltrating the evangelical church from within. This movement gives old theology a fresh face and a new name, and it is hell-bent on reforming the church according to its postmodern dogma."[14] The reference to a "hell-bent" reformation is very intentional: Childers believes these are evil people intent on sowing fatal doctrinal errors into the church.

Once again, even if Childers believes this pastor was generally wrong in his understanding of Christian doctrine, why assume that his motives are corrupt? Christians disagree about

14 Childers, *Another Gospel?* 75.

many things but surely, we should not impute evil intentions to those confessing Christians who disagree with us unless we have some excellent reason to do so. Unfortunately, we do not have access to the pastor to give him an opportunity to defend himself. All we have is Childers' recollection of what he said and how he said it as well as her musings about the underlying motivations. Although we may not have access to the pastor, what we can do is consider Childers' summary of some of his claims and ask a very simple question: is there a charitable interpretation of what the pastor was trying to accomplish, one that does not involve imputing evil motives to him? Might one even find a theological insight in his challenging words?

Let's begin with Childers' scathing summary indictment of the pastor. From there, we will work back through the various claims she tersely summarizes. My goal is to illustrate the extent to which there are indeed generous and perfectly plausible explanations for each of these statements even based on Childers' highly dismissive and polemical recounting of them. Here is her summary:

> Identifying himself as a "hopeful agnostic," this pastor began examining the tenets of the faith. The Virgin Birth? Doesn't matter. The Resurrection? Probably happened, but you don't have to believe in it. The Atonement? That would be a nope. And the Bible? God forbid you believed Scripture was inerrant.[15]

In this passage, we can see five specific claims of concern: the pastor's self-description as a hopeful agnostic, his devaluation of the virgin birth and resurrection, rejection of the atonement, and a denial of biblical inerrancy. Childers clearly believes that these five points illustrate that the pastor was straying from orthodoxy and promoting harmful and subversive teaching.

---

15 Childers, *Another Gospel?* 6.

But need that be the case? Guided by the principle of charity,[16] let's take a closer look at each of those points to see whether there is a more generous interpretation at hand.

Self-identification as a "hopeful agnostic." An agnostic is a person who has no belief as to whether God exists or not. Thus, a pastor who describes himself as a hopeful agnostic would understandably raise eyebrows: after all, surely a pastor is supposed to believe that God *exists*, right? The statement would be even more shocking for a Christian like Childers who defines the foundation of Christianity in terms of Christian doctrine rather than Christ. In that case, to fail to affirm as true those doctrines would constitute a threat to the very *foundation* of Christianity. What is more, conservative Christians like Childers tie belief to a high degree of confidence, if not certainty, in these doctrines. (For further discussion see chapter 5.)

Could there be a plausible sympathetic interpretation of the pastor's provocative self-description? Yes, there certainly is. To begin with, keep in mind that the man is a pastor. Most people are not pastors because they want to be rich and famous. They are pastors because they believe in the mission of God. (Granted, some pastors are out to get rich, but you can usually spot them by their gold rings and Armani suits.) So it is a safe bet that even if the man struggles with belief, his disposition is not one of obstinate disbelief but rather of a struggle with belief as in the desperate father who cries out, "Lord, I believe. Help my unbelief!" (Mark 9:24) Why is the father pleading with Jesus for help with unbelief if he believes? Because sometimes belief is a *struggle*. With that in mind, why not assume that

---

16 The Principle of Charity is a philosophical principle according to which one seeks to understand a speaker in accord with the strongest interpretation of their words. While I agree in general with the principle (indeed, I think it is an implication of the Golden Rule), charity is delimited by plausibility as based on the evidence. For further discussion, see my article "Steelmanning, Strawmanning, and Supermanning," *Tentative Apologist Blog* (March 28, 2022), https://randalrauser.com/2022/03/steelmanning-strawmanning-and-supermanning/

the pastor was simply being honest about his own struggles with belief in the manner of the father in Mark 9?

If you still think the idea of a hopeful agnostic pastor seems contradictory, also keep in mind that good teachers often make points in especially provocative ways that are intended to challenge and destabilize the assumptions of their audience. As such, owning up to one's own doubts with the moniker of a hopeful agnostic is a provocative and memorable way for a pastor to be vulnerable and challenge some deep-seated assumptions about the role that doubt can play in the life of faith.

Just as a marriage is sustained *through* the doubts by the relational commitment of the partners for better or for worse, so it is in the Christian life: belief is important, but it is *not* the foundation. Along these lines, I used to talk about writing a book titled *How to be 100 Percent Christian When You are Only 50 Percent Sure it is True.* I never did write the book, but I still love the title! To conclude, describing oneself as a hopeful agnostic need not be construed as a subversive attack on faith or a devaluation of doctrine. Rather, I would see it simply as an honest recognition of one's own doubts and a provocative and memorable way to reframe the role of doubt in the Christian life.

The Virgin Birth? Doesn't matter. This is one of those points where I really wish we could hear the pastor in his own words. But again, there is a very plausible take on that terse statement: I suspect the pastor is inviting the students to reflect on which doctrines truly are nonnegotiable dogmas and which are not essential to identify with the Christian community.

Let's begin with an interesting fact: one of the leading Protestant theologians of the twentieth century, Wolfhart Pannenberg, rejected the virgin birth of Jesus.[17] Personally, I think he

---

17 For an interesting treatment of Pannenberg's legacy see the obituary in *Christianity Today.* Fred Sanders, "The Strange Legacy of Theologian Wolfhart Pannenberg," *Christianity Today* (September 18, 2014), https://www.

was mistaken when he did this, as I do affirm the doctrine. But here is the point: even though Pannenberg rejected the virgin birth, he accepted other essential doctrines including the Trinity, incarnation, and atonement. Indeed, he gained some fame for his robust evidential defense of the historical resurrection.[18] While there was significant controversy around Pannenberg's rejection of the virgin birth, there simply wasn't a serious debate as to whether he still qualified as a Christian theologian. The fact that Pannenberg was still received as a Christian theologian (indeed, one of the leading Protestant theologians of the twentieth century) provides powerful circumstantial evidence that the virgin birth, while clearly important (it features in the Apostles' Creed, for example) nonetheless functions as a secondary doctrine (in this case, one that supports the incarnation) rather than as an essential dogma in its own right.

By contrast, consider the case of Canadian theologian Greta Vosper. Vosper gained national attention in Canada when the United Church (a large Protestant denomination) undertook a theological inquiry into her ministerial credentials in 2015. The reason: *Vosper had been an outspoken atheist for more than a decade.* Vosper was not happy about this. Indeed, she seemed to view herself as something of a martyr for free thought. She wrote the following on her blog:

> In the last seventeen months, I have learned what the cost of the label atheist is, even here in Canada. My suitability as a minister was not questioned as long as the work I did fell into the realm of "sharing the good news" or preaching something most in liberal churches would call "the way of Jesus"—a work that focuses a community on the values of love, justice,

---

christianitytoday.com/ct/2014/september-web-only/strange-legacy-theologian-wolfhart-pannenberg.html

18 See Pannenberg, *Jesus—God and Man,* trans. Lewis L. Wilkins and Duane A. Priebe (Westminster John Knox Press, 1968).

compassion, and forgiveness. As a non-theist, I was no threat.
As a theological non-realist, I was probably misunderstood.
But as an atheist? How could that be tolerated?[19]

I get it that the final rhetorical question is sarcastic, but I am
inclined to accept the legitimacy of the query: how *could* an
unapologetic atheist pastor be tolerated? Let's be clear: Vosper
was not like a hopeful agnostic pastor who struggles with
unbelief. For her, there was no struggle: she believed God
did not exist, period. Nor did she *want* theism to be true: she
was quite happy as an atheist. I have no problem saying that a
theologian or pastor who is a committed and content atheist
is no longer a *Christian* theologian or pastor. (Alvin Plantinga
used to joke that such individuals are like mountain climbers
who deny the existence of mountains.) By saying this, I take
the stance that the existence of God has an essential dogmatic
status in Christian theological reflection that secondary doctrines like the virgin birth do not. Along those lines, I posted
the following comment on Vosper's blog in response to her
statement that she was being unfairly persecuted:

> While I appreciate your honesty in sharing your atheistic
> convictions, and I recognize that this must be a difficult time,
> the fact remains that you're not being persecuted. Imagine
> if a representative of the Canadian Secular Alliance became
> persuaded of the need to apply Sharia law in society and
> then decided to become vocal in his new convictions. Would
> you think he was being persecuted if the Canadian Secular
> Alliance responded by removing him from being a repre-
> sentative of their organization? Of course not. By endorsing
> Sharia law this individual would have abandoned the very
> raison d'etre for the Canadian Secular Alliance. Since you've
> rejected theism have you not abandoned the very raison d'etre

---

19 Greta Vosper, "The Reason I'm an Atheist," *Greta Vosper Blog* (September
25, 2016), http://www.grettavosper.ca/the-reason-im-an-atheist/

for Christianity? (To be sure, Christianity is far more than theism, but it at least includes theism.) I recognize that you disagree. For you theism is clearly an option. But others within your own church (to say nothing of the rest of Christendom) disagree with you, and one would think they've got a right to see that their church retains its historic commitment to theism, just as the Canadian Secular Alliance has the right to retain its historic commitment to secularism.

To return to the progressive pastor, set against this backdrop I would suspect that his point was not to cast doubt on the virgin birth just for the sake of questioning all that is good and holy. Rather, I take it his point was to get the class thinking about which doctrines truly are the non-negotiable dogmas on which our faith stands or falls, and which are those that we have more freedom to question.

I have that same conversation with the students in my seminary classroom every year. And getting students to think about the status of the virgin birth within the architectonic structure of Christian belief is a good way to begin that challenging conversation.

The Resurrection? Probably happened, but you don't have to believe in it. If you're going to talk about theological hills to die on, surely the historical resurrection of Jesus is one of them, right? The resurrection would certainly seem to belong in the category of dogmatic essentials alongside the existence of God rather than non-essentials like the virgin birth. After all, Paul himself said that if Christ has not been raised then our faith is in vain (1 Corinthians 15:14). So how can a pastor say "you don't have to believe" in the resurrection?

Again, I would love to hear straight from the pastor's mouth what he actually said here because specific nuances can make a world of difference. Since we don't have access to his original words (let alone the intentions behind them), in my attempt to suggest a charitable interpretation, allow me to provide what

I think is a reasonable reconstruction. Let's start with N.T. Wright. A consummate scholar and author of the monumental book *The Resurrection of the Son of God*, Wright is arguably the foremost defender of the historicity of Jesus' resurrection in the world today. So it is safe to say that if anyone appreciates the importance of the resurrection, it is Tom Wright.

Wright was good friends with New Testament scholar Marcus Borg for years until Borg passed away in 2015. In contrast to Wright, Borg was a liberal Christian who didn't accept the historical resurrection of Jesus. Despite that fact, Wright insisted that Borg was still a Christian.[20] (Bet you didn't see that coming!) In a 2006 interview Wright made the following observation: "Marcus Borg really does not believe Jesus Christ was bodily raised from the dead. But I know Marcus well: he loves Jesus and believes in him passionately." Wright then added an explanation for Borg's unbelief: "the philosophical and cultural world he has lived in has made it very, very difficult for him to believe in the bodily resurrection."[21]

Surprising, right? The world's leading defender of the historical resurrection saying that a person who does not accept that historical event can still love Jesus. How can that be? I don't need to tell you that the very idea makes no sense if *doctrine* rather than *relationship* constitutes the Christian's anchor and foundation. However, the matter is different if one begins with relationship.

Let's start by restating the obvious: the resurrection is a central dogma of Christianity. That is *not* in question. And from that I would add that just as with the existence of God, any person who denies the resurrection of Jesus (not simply one who has doubts but one who actually *denies* it) has placed themselves outside of orthodox Christian confession. In this

---

20 For further discussion, see their jointly authored book *The Meaning of Jesus: Two Visions*, 2nd ed. (HarperOne, 2007).

21 Cited in Randal Rauser, *You're Not as Crazy as I Think: Dialogue in a World of Loud Voices and Hardened Opinions* (Biblica, 2011), 124-32.

sense, I would categorize Borg with Vosper rather than with Pannenberg; by denying the resurrection he has placed himself outside the orthodox community of Christian belief. And personally, I would not support an individual who fit that profile for Christian leadership.

However, let's be clear: that is a judgment of ecclesiology (that is, of the governance of the church). It is *not* a judgment of salvation, and it certainly doesn't allow us to conclude that Borg cannot love Jesus. Nor does it mean he would not be welcome to join my congregation on a Sunday morning. Where the status of his unbelief would become relevant is with higher levels of participation such as membership or (as I mentioned above) leadership. But even if I wouldn't support the membership application of an individual who disavowed the resurrection, it doesn't mean I'm saying they are thereby damned, that they don't love Jesus, or that they cannot attend the church.[22]

The real issue is this: can a person who has a theology so unorthodox that they would not be able to be a full participant in the community of faith (e.g. to participate in communion or take on membership), can that person still love Jesus while being wrong about a doctrine that is of central importance to Christianity? Wright seems to think the answer is yes for he says that Borg loves Jesus and believes in him. You might be wondering: what evidence could there *be* for the love of Jesus if one does not believe in his historical resurrection? That's a perfectly reasonable question.

In the case of Borg, we should note first that he had several mystical experiences throughout his life, experiences of the numinous presence of the divine. And these experiences appear to have been central to his particular understanding

---

22 While I would welcome a person to attend church even if they disavowed the resurrection, the situation could change if they were committed to winning over others to their point of view (which is quite a different matter from asking questions and sharing doubts).

of Christ and Christian faith. In his book *Convictions,* Borg describes one of those mystical experiences that he had on a plane flight some years ago when the light around him suddenly began to change:

> It became golden. I looked around, and everything was filled with exquisite beauty—the texture and fabric on the back of the seat in front of me, the tray full of food when it arrived (which I did not eat). Everybody looked beautiful—even a passenger who, as we left Tel Aviv, had struck me as perhaps the ugliest person I had ever seen. He had been pacing the aisle and was so hard to look at that I averted my eyes each time he passed by. Even he looked wondrous. My face was wet with tears. I was filled with joy. I felt that I could live in that state of consciousness forever and it would never grow old. Everything was filled with glory.[23]

Reading Borg, one captures the spirit of the great mystics of the Christian tradition like Meister Eckhart, Catherine of Siena, and Teresa of Avila, people for whom mystical experiences of the numinous were deeply formative for their Christian understanding. So it seems to have been for Borg.

Next, note that Wright invokes what you might call a mitigating factor as regards Borg's unbelief, namely the philosophical and cultural world in which he's lived. Can we say more about this? When it came to Jesus, Borg followed the well-worn practice among biblical scholars of distinguishing between the Jesus of history and the Christ of faith, although his preferred terminology was "Jesus before Easter" and "Jesus after Easter." Borg believed that God was uniquely working in the life of Jesus, but his historical critical perspective left him very skeptical that he could get back by way of history to this

---

23 Borg, *Convictions: How I learned what matters most* (HarperOne, 2014), 38.

Jesus after Easter that he believed he really did experience in his religious life.

In addition, Borg followed a long tradition of scholars like John Robinson and Paul Tillich who reject what Borg calls supernatural theism in favor of a model of panentheism, according to which the world is part of God and God is both transcendent from and radically immanent in the world.[24] This way of thinking has a long pedigree in the Christian tradition,[25] and one of the attractions for Borg is that, in his view, it offers a more adequate balance between God's presence with us and his otherness from us. However, one of the many questionable consequences of panentheistic models of the God/world relation is that they raise skeptical objections about miracles. Because all the world is imbued with the divine, panentheists tend to see all events as, in some sense, miraculous expressions of the divine will. As Friedrich Schleiermacher famously put it, "Miracle is simply the religious name for event."[26] As a result, this view tends to be skeptical of supernaturalist views that see God as intervening in spacetime by way of special miraculous events. This can lead panentheists to adopt a skeptical stance toward specific miracle claims.

These issues are complex, and we can't begin to do them justice here. But that's kind of the point. Before you are too quick to opine on who can love Jesus, you need to understand something about the individual and their story. Wright offers us that caution when speaking about the faith of his close friend Marcus Borg. And I suspect the progressive pastor was likely attempting to facilitate a similar process of critical reflection in his class.

---

24 Borg, *The Heart of Christianity: Rediscovering a Life of Faith* (Harper Collins, 2003), 65 ff.

25 For a helpful overview of thinkers from this tradition see Paul Tillich, *A History of Christian Thought: From Judaic and Hellenistic Origins to Existentialism,* ed. Carl Braaten (Touchstone, 1972).

26 *On Religion: Speeches to Its Cultured Despisers,* trans. John Oman (Westminster John Knox Press, 1994), 88.

The Atonement? That would be a nope. I believe I have a good handle on what happened here because, as I will explain in chapter 8, Childers conflates a particular theory of atonement, the penal substitutionary theory, with the Christian doctrine of atonement. However, the penal substitutionary theory is not itself a doctrine of Christian confession and many Christians reject it. Indeed, the orthodox Christian tradition has never required a specific interpretation of atonement as an object of belief. Consequently, when progressive Christians reject penal substitutionary atonement, they are not thereby rejecting the atonement. Thus, I suspect the pastor was offering a perfectly legitimate critique of a specific theory of atonement, but because Childers has conflated that theory with the doctrine of atonement, she erroneously concluded the pastor had thereby rejected the atonement itself.

And the Bible? God forbid you believed Scripture was inerrant. For starters, *many* Christians reject the doctrine of biblical inerrancy (which is altogether different than rejecting biblical inspiration or authority) so simply rejecting the doctrine is not itself a ground for concern . . . unless you're a conservative evangelical or fundamentalist. But if we are to get a better read on this issue, it would be critical to get the pastor's working definition of inerrancy. Since we don't have access to that, what we can note is that conservative evangelicals have a long history of defending particularly problematic versions of biblical inerrancy. For example, it is not uncommon to find conservative evangelicals arguing that the human biblical authors are without error in all statements they make including matters of science. This is a profoundly misguided notion of inerrancy, however, for the Bible is written against the backdrop of an Ancient Near Eastern science that we do not accept today.[27] When conservative evangelicals insist that the Bible is written without error with regard to all scientific affirmations, they

---

27 For further discussion see Robin Parry, *The Biblical Cosmos: A Pilgrim's Guide to the Weird and Wonderful World of the Bible* (Cascade, 2015).

do not strengthen the credibility and authority of the Bible. On the contrary, they *undermine* that authority even as they are in danger of distorting the text's meaning and significance in an effort to make it fit with contemporary understandings of nature.

To sum up, it is not that hard to identify perfectly charitable interpretations of the progressive pastor's teachings, even based on Childers' terse and rather snarky summary. It appears that he was likely raising some important theological issues and inviting people into deeper reflection on their faith. Perhaps if Childers had stuck around for more than a few months (which is, by the way, a mere 8 percent of the total four-year course of study) rather than dropping out and then summarily writing off the pastor as a tool of the devil, she might have found a greater appreciation for how she could grow in her own faith through participation in the class.

The Process of Deconstruction

Why does Childers respond so negatively when the course clearly impacted her in a positive manner by challenging her to consider the intellectual weakness and spiritual abuse present in her upbringing? We will say a lot more about that question in the next chapter, but for now I want to offer some initial thoughts from the perspective of a professor who has taught in Christian colleges and seminaries for twenty years. Every year, I welcome students into my classes from a variety of Christian backgrounds and educational levels. Each one of them is invited into a journey of theological reflection and growth. But undoubtedly, that process brings some surprises along the way, challenges that the student did not anticipate.

I would argue that for many the biggest surprise is coming to terms with the process of education itself. You see, students commonly assume that the process of theological learning is all about *addition*, as if they start the semester with a partially built brick wall of prior understanding, and then week by week, lecture by lecture, reading by reading, assignment by assignment, the course will simply add more bricks to that wall. While education certainly is concerned with adding new understanding rather like placing new bricks on a pre-existing wall, that is only part of the story. The other part of the process is just as critical, and it involves challenging old understandings and thus *removing faulty bricks*. That process is popularly known as *deconstruction,* and it is the complement to the positive *constructive* side of education. To put it simply, the process of learning is as much about *renovating old structures* as *adding new ones.*

Deconstruction can be very difficult, especially when you are not prepared for it in advance. If you are particularly attached to a brick wall that you have built up over the years, it can be deeply disconcerting to have people fiddling with it. As a result, the process of deconstruction can be painful and not all students handle it well. In rare cases, it can even foment an existential crisis.

I remember one student who enrolled in seminary some years ago: I'll call him Bill. Bill started passionate about the Bible and excited to learn so that he could become more effective at teaching Sunday school. But after a few weeks, he came to my office disillusioned. Bill was learning things about the Bible that were upsetting long held beliefs he had been taught in his church and he was feeling threatened. In short, the professor was challenging Bill to remove some bricks and he didn't like that at all. I encouraged Bill to persevere, noting that the process of deconstruction could be painful and difficult. But I told him if he stuck with it, he would get to a point of experiencing some exciting new construction in his understanding. Bill seemed unconvinced but he half-heartedly agreed to continue with his classes. However, when I heard from him again a month later, the tone had shifted. Bill sent me a brief email in which he tersely stated he had decided he was done with seminary, and he would be withdrawing before the end of the semester. Sometimes the old pile of bricks is tough to give up.

In twenty years of teaching, that is one of the more extreme cases I have seen of a student who reacted negatively to the process of deconstruction. But if anything, Childers' response to the progressive pastor is even more extreme. Not only did she withdraw from the class, but she wrote a whole book about the experience! What is more, she repeatedly challenges not only the doctrine of the pastor and fellow students, but she also judges their hearts by insisting that they have malicious intentions and stand in opposition to God and his kingdom.

Leaving an educational process during deconstruction can be a bit like leaving the operating theater in the midst of surgery: it's always better to wait until you're stitched back up! Sadly, I fear that by leaving seminary mid-semester, Bill never had the benefit of reconstruction: his impatience did him no favors. I suspect it is a similar case for Childers. Leaving a four-year process only four months in, which as I said is a mere 8 percent of the total course of study, would've exposed Childers to some significant early deconstruction of her understanding but with little time to process these challenges or to begin placing new bricks. Consequently, this would predictably only magnify the negativity of the experience and likely lead to blowback against those who facilitated the experience in the first place.

When students cannot handle the process of deconstruction, it is not uncommon to project nefarious intentions on the teacher: it must be their fault! In a sense, the reaction is understandable: after all, when education seems to lack a point beyond introducing cognitive dissonance and thus disorientation about received modes of understanding, it is natural to conclude that the instructor is the problem and the act may be borne of malice. However, at its core this response looks rather like a case of *shooting the messenger*. If there are flawed or weak parts of your understanding, then the removal of faulty bricks is necessary for genuine and long-lasting growth. And I would submit that any hostility should rather be directed toward those who gave you an education that needed deconstruction in the first place. Attacking those who instigate the process of deconstruction that is necessary to clear the way for new learning is equivalent to tossing the contractor out of your house for ripping up a rotten floor in preparation for new renovations.

In *Another Gospel?* Childers does not hold back on impugning the pastor and his motives. She insists that he was not really engaged on a good-faith journey to grow deeper in his Christian faith and to help others to do so as well. Rather, she insists that "he had a bone to pick with Christianity."[28] Retreating to a simplistic tableau of heroes and villains that recasts the pastor as a bad guy may effectively externalize and so neutralize the threat, but it does so at the cost of both truth and basic Christian charity.

---

28 Childers, *Another Gospel?* 6.

2

The Binary Mindset
of Conservative Evangelicalism

Childers believes the progressive pastor was not a real Christian. Instead, he was a tool of the evil one, maliciously out to undermine her faith. Nor does she believe that this pastor represented a unique threat to the faith. As she puts it, this kind of "unorthodox thinking" had been tried before and it "had been refuted a hundred times over since the invention of the pen." Despite that fact, this unorthodox thinking keeps coming back. Why? Childers likens it to the tares sown among the good wheat in Jesus' parable. Needless to say, it is the devil who sows false teachings and anti-Christian agents in the midst of God's wheat: "wheat and tares, true ideas and false ideas have grown together throughout church history, and it's up to faithful Christians to be watchful and diligent to compare every idea with the Word of God and see if it lines up."[29]

As if that weren't insulting enough, Childers also compares the pastor and his teaching to a wolf out to consume unsuspecting prey. And she reminds us that "Jesus predicted that

29 Childers, *Another Gospel?* 94. Cf. 97.

wolves would invade his church."[30] Whether it is the tare that looks like wheat or the wolf that looks like sheep, we should remember that "True Christians and false Christians will live together in the same world . . . ."[31] And we should be prepared to identify and out the deceivers lest we be tricked by them.

In the previous chapter, I provided an initial explanation of this abrupt switch from viewing the pastor as a Christ follower, friend, and spiritual leader to a subversive enemy. I suggested that it reflected predictable blowback to the existential struggle created by deconstruction and exacerbated by a process shut down midstream. In this chapter, I want to explore this dynamic further by considering the extent to which Childers' reaction provides evidence of a specifically binary mindset that is characteristic of conservative evangelicalism and fundamentalism. According to that mindset, the world is divided into stark categories of good and evil, right and wrong, light and darkness, truth and error.

When individuals begin to challenge the binary mindset, it can start to fracture in the face of the inevitable shades of grey that exist all around us. However, as in the case of a blowback from failed deconstruction, the binary mindset can respond to challenges by reasserting itself with even greater force, the binary options now reinforced and even more resistant to challenge. The sad thing about this reactive process is that those who opt to retreat further into their binary mindset thereby are left unable to acknowledge either the truth in opposing views or the weaknesses in their own. Rather than growing in understanding, they withdraw further into the space of indoctrination. It seems to me that this is the phenomenon that we find present time and again in *Another Gospel?* Rather than welcome the challenges of the progressive pastor and his classroom and seek to learn from them, Childers opts to retreat into a reinforced binary mindset.

---

30 Childers, *Another Gospel?* 99.

31 Childers, *Another Gospel?* 98.

As this chapter begins, I first want to say something more about the binary mindset, how it appears to assert itself in Childers, and some of the ways that it is challenged from a Christian worldview. Next, I will consider how the binary mindset feeds into a culture war mentality that provides fertile soil for growing conservative evangelical and fundamentalist ministries that draw their vibrancy by defining themselves over-against perceived enemies. This leads to the ironic situation in which Childers chides others for heresy hunting even as she engages in precisely that behavior.

The Binary Mindset

I said in the last chapter that I can understand something of where Childers is coming from because I, too, was raised in a conservative evangelical Christian church. One particular anecdote captures the mindset with which I was raised. At one point, I became convinced that I had to destroy my secular music if I was seriously going to follow Jesus. And that meant smashing my favorite Beach Boys cassette on the driveway. I reasoned that if you're not singing for God you're singing for the devil. And since "Surfin' USA" did not reference God, there was only one category left: Brian Wilson and crew were on the side of the evil one. Indeed, if anything, the beautiful harmonies in songs like "God Only Knows" and "Good Vibrations" were simply further evidence of the devil's wiles as an angel of light. And so, the cassette met its fateful end as it splintered into the concrete of the driveway and my own binary mindset.[32]

The binary picture of this worldview was further enhanced by my conviction in the imminent end of the world and the belief that the devil is a liar who even now operates actively to deceive people and trick them in whatever manner possible. That left me on guard seeking the devil's stamp in all sorts of

---

32 For my story see Randal Rauser, *What's So Confusing About Grace?* (2 Cup Press, 2017), 58 ff.

otherwise neutral cultural expressions. Whether it was the entrancing melodies of "Good Vibrations" or the allure of a pastor who offers some new teaching to tickle the ears, you needed to be on guard for the devil subtly working in all sorts of unexpected ways. Like those tares that look dangerously like wheat or the wolf who is dressed up as a sheep, the world is full of malevolent deceptions ready to pull us down into darkness. So be watchful!

The binary mindset offers a real allure for conservative Christians because at first blush it can seem very biblical. For one thing, it fits into that expectation of an imminent end of the world, a cosmic battle between good and evil, and the role of the devil as a consummate liar seeking to deceive and lead us into darkness. And if one reads the Bible looking for validation of a simple binary mindset, one can definitely find it. (Of course, with sufficient determination one can validate pretty much any opinion in the Bible, so take that for what you will.)

When it comes to binary categories, there is perhaps no better place to go than the words of Jesus in the Gospel of John. Jesus is the man of truth who opposes the lies of the devil and his followers (8:44). Jesus is the true light (1:9) and those who walk with him walk in the light (8:12). But people loved darkness because their deeds are evil (3:19) and they walk in darkness. Those who are in Christ have eternal life but those who are outside Christ face death (5:24). Add it up and you have a stark choice: truth vs. lies, light vs. darkness, life vs. death. And everyone you meet is classified on one side or the other.

While we should remain committed to distinguishing truth from lies, light from darkness, and life from death, the reality is that contrary to this binary mindset, we often encounter these categories not in black and white but rather a mixture of greys. And there is a distinct twofold danger when you adopt a binary mindset that persists in dividing all positions and persons into the simple categories of truth vs. lies, light vs. darkness, and life vs. death.

The first thing to note is that most people are subject to an optimism bias in which they tend to think more favorably about themselves than the evidence warrants. And that means that most people will be inclined to place themselves on the side of truth, light, and life and outsiders to their group on the side of lies, darkness, and death. Once that happens, your ability to introspect critically on your status and character will be critically hampered. Yet, we should not under-estimate our ability to self-deceive. In the words of Jeremiah, "The heart is deceitful above all things and beyond cure" (Jeremiah 17:9). And as Paul warned the Corinthians, "Examine yourselves to see whether you are in the faith; test yourselves. Do you not realize that Christ Jesus is in you—unless, of course, you fail the test?" (2 Corinthians 13:5)

One of the most disturbing reminders for the need to self-introspect is found in Jesus' haunting parable of the sheep and goats (Matthew 25:31-46). Reading through this unsettling passage, one thing becomes clear: some sheep are surprised to discover they are sheep, and some goats are surprised to discover they are goats. That ought to give all of us a resonant caution about drawing too simple and straight a line between insiders on the side of truth, light, and life and outsiders on the side of lies, darkness, and death. Harry Blamires put it like this:

> the Christian mind cannot accept the facile distinction made by the secular mind—reflected in public society—between the nation's criminals and libertines on the one hand and her good men on the other. For the discerning Christian knows that a cunning or intelligent man may lead a life of almost diabolical pride, in which he strives in every moment to minister to the desires and vanities of his own inflated self—and yet may pass for a respectable, law-abiding citizen. Indeed he may rise to a position of eminence in the world

by the persistent and subtle practice of the most calculated self-service. He may become a judge, packing off poor men to gaol [jail] with words of stern condemnation ostensibly reflecting the indignation of righteous men, and yet he may be, by virtue of a cancerous inner self-centredness, the greatest sinner, essentially the most evil man, ever to have entered the courtroom in which he sits—though its dock has accommodated a stream of murders, thieves, and perverts for the last fifty years. The Christian mind cannot overlook this possibility.[33]

Blamires may have framed the lesson in the language of the courtroom, but we can apply it equally to the church. You could be a preeminent Christian leader according to Childers' dictates as to what doctrines and practices identify such a leader and you may dedicate your life to calling out Christians who don't measure up to your standard, insisting that they are fakers, tares, and wolves. And yet, all the while you could be the greatest sinner and a more doctrinally confused person than the long history of "heretics" you effectively condemned to theological exile and damnation. The Christian mind cannot overlook *that* possibility either.

The other side of this coin is equally important: just as we need to remain aware of the degree to which we can fall victim to lies, darkness, and death, so we need to be attentive to the degree to which perceived outsiders can live in accord with truth, light, and life. Failure to recognize that fact inhibits our ability to learn from and be changed by these "outsiders" and the truth, light, and life they may have to share with us. Consequently, getting locked into a binary mindset becomes a sort of double whammy, one which both inhibits our ability to introspect the weakness or error in our own views even as it also undercuts our ability to recognize the strength and truth in others.

---

33 *The Christian Mind* (SPCK, 1963), 90.

While I was raised with a Christian conservative evangelical binary mindset, I gradually deconstructed it some years ago. Since then, I have become more intentional about attempting to discern where I am falling victim to lies, darkness, and death and where those I am inclined to view as outsiders are actually the unexpected heralds of truth, light, and life.[34] By contrast, it seems to me that Childers remains very much locked into that binary mindset and it frames her entire way of thinking about progressive Christianity, thereby inhibiting her own introspection and her ability to engage charitably with and thus learn from dissenting perspectives.

The first piece of evidence for the binary mindset is in the title of Childers' book. After being challenged by the progressive pastor, Childers immediately falls into a binary alternative: either he is proclaiming the one true evangel, or he is presenting *another* gospel. The binary comes into broader relief with the subtitle: *A Lifelong Christian Seeks Truth in Response to Progressive Christianity*. In other words, Christian Truth versus the implied falsehoods of Progressive Christianity. The clear implication from the outset is that there is *no truth* to be found in progressive Christianity and thus *nothing* to learn from it. These are only enemies to be outed and opposed and false ideas to be defeated.

As I noted in chapter 1, Childers acknowledges multiple weaknesses in her Christian upbringing including a lack of theological and apologetic foundation for her beliefs and the spiritual and emotional abuse that came with particular teaching about hell and eternity. Even though the progressive pastor's course enabled her to become more aware of some of these weaknesses, she cannot acknowledge the extent to which

---

34 One of the ways I seek to do this is by participating in devil's advocate debates in which I commit to arguing the opposite of my personal views. See, for example, my devil's advocate debate with leading atheist Michael Ruse on the popular apologetics show "Unbelievable," https://www.premierchristianradio. com/Shows/Saturday/Unbelievable/Episodes/Unbelievable-Devil-s-Advocate-Debate-Michael-Ruse-the-theist-vs-Randal-Rauser-the-atheist

the course enabled her wrestling with God. Instead, Childers exhibits a common trait of the binary mindset: *question motives and impugn character*. In other words, when people from the outgroup challenge your beliefs, you neutralize the challenge by framing it as arising from a wicked character which is seeking to delude you from the truth.

This stark response appears in Strobel's foreword when he opts to characterize the views of progressive Christians not only as errors but as "subtle *deceptions*."[35] Childers likewise adopts this uncharitable moral framing: "In class," she says, "I felt as if the pastor was presenting himself as just another sheep, humbly seeking truth and pursing God."[36] However, when she concluded that he was wrong, she did not seriously countenance the possibility that he might be a shepherd who made some honest mistakes. Instead, she now concludes that he should be classed as a malevolent wolf in shepherd's clothing.[37]

Time and again, Childers adopts this framework for interpreting those with whom she disagrees. She assumes that the pastor had them read a book by Brian McLaren not because they might be able to learn from it but simply to spot "deception."[38] And when she encounters the teaching of Franciscan Richard Rohr, once again her only categories are to consider either that he is correct or he is engaged in malicious deception: "So is Richard Rohr correct in saying that a view of God that includes punishment and reward is evidence of a toxic mind in need of deep healing? Or is this nothing more than a manipulative trick—a type of spiritual gaslighting—meant to make one question their mental health if they disagree with him?"[39] Childers doesn't even consider the other options

---

35 Strobel, "Foreword," in Childers, *Another Gospel?* xiv, emphasis added.

36 Childers, *Another Gospel?* 99.

37 Childers, *Another Gospel?* 100.

38 Childers, *Another Gospel?* 23.

39 Childers, *Another Gospel?* 185.

including *maybe Rohr is at least possibly right* and *maybe Rohr is honestly wrong*. Time and again, every idea, position, and person is forced through a binary grid: either truth, light, and life or lies, darkness, and death.

This simple binary mindset also heightens the crisis that Childers experiences when her understanding is challenged. For example, she had been raised with no real awareness of textual biblical criticism. And so, when questions about the origin of the biblical text are first raised to her and she is forced to consider the degree to which the Bible is a properly *human* collection of writings, she does not consider that the Bible might be God's divine word with the smudges of human fingerprints. Instead, she is locked into binary options: either the Bible is completely without error in the manner she had always supposed or "*Is everything I've ever believed about him a lie?*"[40] Again, the vast middle ground is not even an option.

The further you read in *Another Gospel?* the more disturbing and dehumanizing is the rhetoric against Childers' progressive enemies. For example, consider the following passage in which she goes on at some length about the pastor who led the course as one of the "ravenous wolves" of Matthew 7:15-16:

> These teachers would look like sheep, talk like sheep, walk like sheep, and act like sheep. But these sheepy-looking beasts wouldn't be looking to snack on grass and clover. These would be carnivorous hunters looking to sink their chops into a nice juicy sheep steak. While wheat and tares represent true believers and false ones, a predatory wolf is a whole different animal. This can be especially confusing for the flock when the wolf in question is dressed up as a shepherd—the one person with whom the sheep are conditioned to feel safe. In class, I felt as if the pastor was presenting himself as just another sheep, humbly seeking truth and pursuing God. In

---

40 Childers, *Another Gospel?* 3. She also says "I could be holding in my hands an accurate copy of *a lie.*" *Another Gospel?* 133. Cf. 140.

the beginning I believed him. I thought we were on the same page. And because he was my "shepherd" who had won my respect and trust, I let my guard down.[41]

It is important to underscore just how disturbing this passage is. This pastor who led a course that revealed some deep problems in Childers' Christian upbringing is labeled a "predatory wolf," one who is aiming to deceive "the sheep" by acting as if he is "just another sheep". In this way, he gets them "conditioned to feel safe" and gains their "respect and trust," all as preparation for the moment when he plans to sink his "chops into a nice juicy sheep steak." Goodness me, this rhetoric is really running wild, isn't it?

Remember the famous Abraham Maslow quote: to the man with a hammer, everything looks like a nail. And to the person with a simple binary mindset of truth vs. lies, light vs. darkness and life vs. death, every person who is not deemed to be on the side of truth, light, and life is objectified and outed as a malevolent, ravenous foe.

Enemies build Ministries

Clint Eastwood's film *Flags of Our Fathers* tells the story of the famous flag-raising photo taken on Mount Suribachi during World War 2. In the film we learn how this iconic image was staged to promote the war bonds effort all while concealing disturbing facts about the war from the American public. The propagandistic use of this image is justified by the army to the end of inspiring Americans to join in the cause. As one soldier observes plaintively, "We need easy to understand truths and damn few words." [42] In short, don't give us ethical nuance

---

41 Childers, *Another Gospel?* 99-100.

42 This example is discussed in Rauser, *You're Not as Crazy as I Think,* 29-30.

when we need people buying war bonds! It is for good reason that the old saying identifies truth as the first casualty of war.

The binary mindset is perfect for wartime because it ensures that we have clearly defined "good guys" and "bad guys." In that way, we know whom to shoot at and whom to protect and we are united in the rightness of our cause and the wrongness of the foe. As journalist Chris Hedges astutely observes in his book *War is a Force that Gives Us Meaning*,[43] war provides a powerful way to galvanize disparate groups with a shared purpose united against a common enemy.

Not surprisingly, there is no shortage of military styled language in the Bible for those who are looking for it. Think, for example, of Paul's description of Christians as soldiers (Philippians 2:25) or his declaration that "We demolish arguments and every pretension that sets itself up against the knowledge of God, and we take captive every thought to make it obedient to Christ." (2 Corinthians 10:5) There is a war to win and as we fight on the side of truth, light, and life, we are united against a common enemy that we must defeat!

The same social dynamic that can unify societies and militaries in battle can also unite Christian churches and fledgling ministries. I capture that dynamic in the following maxim: *enemies build ministries.* As we fight the cause of the Lord against the world of flesh and the devil, we are spurred on by the rightness of our cause and the need to demolish the enemy. In the same way that politicians who appeal to stark binary categories and invoke simplistic slogans are often rewarded with election to office, and generals who invoke start categories of good and evil motivate troops, sell war bonds, and win battles, so Christian ministries, authors, and speakers who appeal to binary categories are often rewarded with spiking book sales and soaring donations. The common enemy galvanizes the audience and unites those in the ministry with a clear, common purpose.

---

43 *War is a Force that Gives Us Meaning* (PublicAffairs, 2014).

So it is with Childers' framing of her book as a response to *another* gospel, one which she warns is even now being surreptitiously introduced into churches like the tares sown into the wheat or the wolf slavering to bite into some sheep steaks.

It appears that Childers' book has become very successful. As of April 2022, two years after publication, there are 2590 reviews (and counting) on Amazon.com averaging five stars. And as I write, Childers' next book is scheduled for release in October 2022.[44] In the last few years, Childers has become an in-demand public speaker at churches and conferences. She also runs a popular podcast[45] and even has an entire premium online course titled "Responding to Progressive Christianity," which is devoted to guarding the flock against the alleged errors of predatory progressives, and all for $249.[46]

To be sure, I don't begrudge anyone's success. My point here is that there is a ready audience for material that is presented in the terms of a binary mindset as it unites people against a common enemy and imbues them with a sense of shared purpose and confidence in the rightness of their cause. But as with war, when we adopt this binary mindset truth is the first casualty.

An Ironic, Hyperfundamentalist, Heresy Hunting Conclusion

I stated at the beginning of the chapter that the binary mindset keeps one both from careful self-introspection that would reveal the weaknesses in one's own position as well as the degree to which there are legitimate and important insights

---

44 Childers, *Live Your Truth and Other Lies: Exposing Popular Deceptions That Make Us Anxious, Exhausted, and Self-Obsessed* (Tyndale Momentum, 2022).

45 https://www.alisachilders.com/podcast.html

46 https://www.onlinechristiancourses.com/ occ-progressive-christianity-self-paced-course/

in the views of others. The ironic way that this affects Childers is evident in chapter 4 when she takes aim at what she calls "hyperfundamentalism." According to Childers, this is a particularly aggressive and anti-intellectual sectarian expression of Christianity which encourages people to engage in heresy hunting. As she puts it, heresy hunters have an unhealthy interest in identifying "false teachers" and they "delight in pointing fingers."[47] Childers insists that she opposes this unsavory activity for it fails in the love of neighbor. As she observes, "I try to give as much grace as possible to Christians who disagree with me on issues that don't directly affect salvation."[48]

The lack of self-awareness here is, frankly, stunning. Thus far, we have seen Childers locked in a sharp binary mindset according to which either the progressive Christian outsiders are offering a completely true and good insight, or they are a malevolent wolf out to eat the hapless sheep. From that starting point, she flips to the second interpretation in short order, dismissing progressive Christians as wolves, tares, fake Christians, and deceivers who seek to sell "another gospel." But that's not all: in subsequent chapters we will see her pile on additional charges including claims that progressive Christians reject objective truth, the atonement, and hell. Along the way, she shall also accuse them of specific heresies including Gnosticism and Marcionism.

How is it that Childers can show a clear awareness of the problem of heresy hunting but then conveniently exempt herself from the offending behavior when she perfectly fits the profile? On the one hand, one could say this is simply a predictable manifestation of Childers' inability to introspect about her own position or accept insight from those in the otherized outgroups. At the same time, there may be something more at play here as well. Consider again her words: "I try to give as much grace as possible to *Christians* who

---

47 Childers, *Another Gospel?* 63.

48 Childers, *Another Gospel?* 63.

disagree with me on issues that don't directly affect salvation." At first blush this statement invoking grace appears to endorse generosity toward those with whom you disagree. But look again: Childers explicitly restricts this generosity to *people she considers to be Christians*. As we have seen, she is clear that in her view, progressive Christians do not belong in that group: that is, they are not really Christians at all. And since they are not Christians, it follows as a result, that they don't qualify to receive that same level of charitable engagement.

They *are* the enemy after all, and there is a war to be won.

3

Progressive Christianity
is Not a New Religion

*A*nother *Gospel?* has more than its share of stunning and profoundly uncharitable claims. I'm still thinking about the description of progressive pastors as ravenous wolves "looking to sink their chops into a nice juicy sheep steak." Ick, that image is going to be tough to shake. But as bad as that is, it may be that the single most shocking claim of all is the one at the center of the book, namely that progressive Christians are not Christians at all but rather fakers. And the gospel they proclaim is altogether different from *the* Gospel. Indeed, it represents an altogether distinct religion created by the evil one, crafted to lead good people into darkness. As Childers says, "It's an entirely different religion—with another Jesus—and another gospel."[49] Shocking in its absoluteness, that statement perfectly encapsulates the binary mindset.

In this chapter, I want to offer a response to that extraordinary claim. To that end, we will proceed in three parts. To begin with, I want to consider five specific individuals that

---

49 Childers, *Another Gospel?* 76.

Childers targets in the book. She classifies each of these individuals as a progressive Christian and thus, by her measure, a tare, a wolf, and a fake Christian. I will offer an evaluation of the public evidence for each of those claims. Next, I will include the highlights of an interview I had with one of those individuals, Peter Enns. After that, I will challenge the binary mindset with an extended river-borne metaphor courtesy of Brian McLaren. I will conclude the chapter by pointing out that progressive Christianity is not a new religion but rather an *ad hoc* collective of people brought together with the simple goal of growing in their mutual understanding much like a theology classroom.

A Brief Look at Five "Progressive Christians"

If Childers had limited her analysis of progressive Christianity to vague anonymous interlocutors from her past like the shadowy progressive pastor, it would've been more challenging to issue a final verdict. Fortunately, she makes the task significantly easier insofar as she identifies multiple well-known individuals as progressive Christians including Brian McLaren, William Paul Young, Tony Jones, Nadia Bolz-Weber, Peter Enns, Brian Zahnd, Rachel Held Evans, Richard Rohr, Steve Chalke, and John Pavlovitz. What I want to do in this section is offer an evaluation of her claim that progressive Christianity is not Christianity at all by considering the religious status of five of those individuals: Enns, Zahnd, Evans, Rohr, and Pavlovitz. I believe that survey will be sufficient to put to rest Childers' stunningly audacious claim that these individuals are not Christians.

Peter Enns has been a friend for close to a decade now and I'll be straight up with you: I'm very much convinced that he's a Christian. Moreover, I'm clearly not the only one. Enns taught for years at the conservative Reformed Westminster Theological Seminary and while he eventually left the school over a doctrinal disagreement, the issue was *never* over whether Enns should be considered a Christian. Rather, the matter concerned whether his 2005 book *Inspiration and Incarnation* was consistent with the Westminster Confession of Faith, a Reformed Protestant confessional statement from 1646. I hope you can appreciate that within the vastness of Christendom, that's a very particular issue over which to be debating.

After leaving Westminster, Enns became the Abram S. Clemens Professor of Biblical Studies at Eastern University, an evangelical Christian undergraduate institution. Among his other Christian affiliations, Enns has also served in the past as a senior fellow at Biologos, an evangelical Christian organization that promotes the dialogue between Neo-Darwinian evolution and Christian faith. Enns has also been granted book awards by *Christianity Today* and the Evangelical Christian Publishers Association, both of which tend not to grant awards to non-Christian authors who are seeking to undermine the one true faith. (I admit it: I'm starting to lapse into sarcasm. But if God can be sarcastic (e.g. Job 38:21), perhaps I can too.)

As a full professor at Eastern University, Enns affirms the school's Doctrinal Statement which is a thoroughly evangelical Christian statement of belief that includes confessions of Scripture, God, salvation, the sacraments/ordinances, and the church.[50] Further, faculty at Eastern are required to sign this doctrinal statement annually and the only exemption allowed pertains to the mode of water baptism. Finally, Enns has attended an Episcopalian church for several years.

To sum up, Enns identifies as a Christian and is recognized as such by leading institutions like Westminster Theological Seminary, Eastern University, Biologos, *Christianity Today,* and the Evangelical Christian Publishers Association, not to mention the many thousands of Christians who read his books and listen to his very popular podcast *The Bible for Normal*

---

50 https://www.eastern.edu/about/vision-mission-faith/
what-we-believe-doctrinal-statement

People. Suffice it to say, the suggestion that he is actually a malevolent adherent of a distinct religion looks on its face to be a bald piece of slander.

Brian Zahnd is the author of several popular books on Christian theology and spirituality including *Sinners in the Hands of a Loving God* (I love that title!) and *A Farewell to Mars*. Zahnd has also written essays for *Christianity Today*.[51] Perhaps most importantly, for over forty years he has been the lead pastor of Word of Life Church, a non-denominational Christian Church in St. Joseph, Missouri. When you've been the lead pastor of a church for forty years, one can safely assume that your beliefs are consistent with the church's confessions. So what is Word of Life's confessional statement? At the church's website there are two statements of doctrine listed: the Apostles' Creed and the Nicene Creed.[52] These are good choices for those concerned with orthodoxy given that they are the two most universal creeds in the history of the church. And that clearly points to the fact that Word of Life, and by extension Zahnd himself, are located squarely within the mainstream orthodox tradition.

In June 2021, I interacted with Zahnd on Twitter at which time I made him aware of Childers' claim that he was a progressive Christian and that progressive Christians allegedly aren't Christians at all. Zahnd replied that he rejected the identifier "progressive Christian" altogether. Instead, he located himself squarely within the ecumenical creedal tradition that has guided his church for forty years: "I'm not a progressive Christian—just ask progressive Christians. And neither am I a conservative Christian—just ask conservative Christians.

---

51 See for example, Brian Zahnd, "Beauty Will Save the World: Rediscovering the allure and mystery of Christianity," *Christianity Today* (February 27, 2012), https://www.christianitytoday.com/ct/2012/february/excerpt-beauty-world.html "You Are What You Pray," *Christianity Today* (June 3, 2013), https://www.christianitytoday.com/pastors/2013/june-online-only/you-are-what-you-pray.html

52 https://wolc.com/who-we-are/what-we-believe/

I am a (small o) orthodox Christian."[53] Zahnd concluded
our exchange by offering this incisive quote as a response to
Childers' extreme claims: "When you label me, you negate
me."[54] In other words, the kind of irresponsible labeling that
Childers was engaged in serves only to distort and then dismiss those with whom one disagrees rather than charitably
engaging them and what they actually believe.

Rachel Held Evans was raised evangelical in Dayton, Tennessee and wrote about matters of Christian faith from the
place of someone coming to terms with a history of living in
the Bible Belt. Along the way, she offered penetrating insights
and many incisive critiques of conservative evangelicalism in
several popular books, perhaps most notably the *New York
Times* bestseller *A Year of Biblical Womanhood.*

Evans was originally evangelical, but she ceased identifying
herself as such due to the increasing politicization of the religious right that manifested itself in ever growing support for
Donald Trump. After that, she identified as Episcopalian and
attended St. Luke's Episcopal Church in Cleveland, Tennessee,
a church which is rooted in the Book of Common Prayer and
has a statement of faith that is sourced in the triune God, the
reconciling work of Christ, and Scripture.[55]

Tragically, Evans passed away unexpectedly in 2019. After
her passing, *Christianity Today* published an obituary by John
Stonestreet. As *Christianity Today* editor Mark Galli observed,
the magazine wanted an essay that would "properly honor her
without pretending she didn't have significant disagreements
with important CT distinctives." In other words, the point of
the obituary was not to attack Evans and it was most certainly
not to question her Christian faith. Rather, it was meant to
honor her memory with an honest and irenic recounting of

53 https://twitter.com/BrianZahnd/status/1414050887027380231, emphasis
added.

54 https://twitter.com/BrianZahnd/status/1414050887027380231

55 https://www.stlukescleveland.org/we-believe

theological difference between her stance and the more conservative orientation of *Christianity Today.*

Even so, the obituary was not well received, and many
Christians interpreted the critique as rather mean-spirited.
As the furor began to build, Galli took on the controversy by
admitting in an essay that *Christianity Today* had failed. In
his *mea culpa* he first highlighted the marvelous legacy that
Evans left behind: "I've heard stories of how she helped so
many grapple with their faith, as well as her continual focus on
Jesus. Evans was admired by many for good reasons."[56] While
he also appreciated Stonestreet's essay, Galli could understand
why many *Christianity Today* readers found it to be overly
critical. And for that, he apologized. Galli concluded his essay
by describing Evans as a "dynamic sister in Christ."

Once again, while there have been Christians who disagreed
with Evans on one or another matter, *nobody* in the mainstream
conversation has ever doubted that she was actually a Christian.
Her books and blog were beloved by hundreds of thousands
of Christians, she was lauded by *Christianity Today*, and she
remained a faithful Episcopalian to her passing.

Richard Rohr is a Franciscan friar who is deeply imbued
with the Christian mystical tradition. He is the author of
several popular books including *The Universal Christ: How
a Forgotten Reality Can Change Everything We See, Hope
For, and Believe.* Rohr ministers at the Center for Action and
Contemplation, a retreat center in New Mexico. And like many
in the Christian mystical tradition from Meister Eckhart to
Teresa of Avila to Thomas Merton, he has his critics. However,
the Center's website offers this statement on Rohr's doctrine:

> Father Richard is an orthodox Catholic Christian, who is in
> good standing with Rome, the Archbishop of Santa Fe, and

---

56 Mark Galli, "RE: Rachel Held Evans," *Christianity Today* (May 8, 2019),
https://www.christianitytoday.com/ct/2019/may-web-only/re-rachel-held-ev-
ans.html

his own Franciscan superiors. He deeply believes the most traditional and orthodox Christian beliefs like the Trinity, the Incarnation, the Body of Christ, the Eucharist, the Perennial Tradition of both the Eastern and Western Churches, Biblical spirituality, and The Divine Indwelling of the Holy Spirit—and he tries to present all of these in pastoral and prayerful ways that make sense to 21st century sincere seekers.[57]

As with our other examples, Rohr may be more "liberal" than some folk (and more conservative than others), but it cannot plausibly be claimed that he is an adherent of an entirely different religion when he remains a professing Catholic in good standing with his church.

John Pavlovitz, our final example, is a bit more complicated. To begin with, he started out as a Christian pastor who worked for years at several Methodist churches. However, a pivotal moment came in 2013 when he was fired by a church for not fitting into their theological and cultural ethos. Since then, Pavlovitz has gained renown (or notoriety, depending on your perspective) by offering theological musings and sharp criticisms of evangelical Christianity in his popular blog "Stuff that Needs to be Said."[58] Among his recent targets, Pavlovitz has taken on the evangelical love for Donald Trump and guns along with the high suspicion evangelicals have of refugees.[59,60] Pavlovitz's most recent book is titled *If God is Love, Don't be a Jerk: Finding a Faith That Makes Us Better Humans*,[61] and

---

57 https://cac.org/about/richard-rohr/

58 https://johnpavlovitz.com/

59 Amanda Abrams, "How Raleigh's John Pavlovitz Went from Fired Megachurch Pastor to Rising Star of the Religious Left," *Indy Week* (November 22, 2017), https://indyweek.com/news/raleigh-s-john-pavlovitz-went-fired-megachurch-pastor-rising-star-religious-left/

60 See, for example, "If Migrants were Handguns," *Stuff that Needs to be Said* (August 19, 2019), https://johnpavlovitz.com/2019/08/19/if-migrants-were-handguns/

61 (Westminster John Knox Press, 2021).

it has received a ringing endorsement from Christian leader Shane Claiborne.

I said that Pavlovitz began as a Methodist. However, for the last few years he has done some speaking/preaching at Unitarian Universalist congregations. It is not clear to me whether Pavlovitz himself identifies as a Unitarian Universalist or whether he simply has occasion to speak in their meetings. After all, I once participated in a dialogue on the existence of God at a Unitarian Universalist church. It didn't follow that I adhered to their beliefs.

Speaking of beliefs, some people would classify Unitarian Universalism as a liberal Christian denomination. Others might classify it as a distinct religion. While Unitarian Universalists have no creed or scripture and welcome people from a wide diversity of theological perspectives in their community, the uniting core value of Unitarian Universalist communities is a commitment to the inherent dignity and value of all persons. However, given that Unitarian Universalism has such minimal requirements in terms of belief and practice, it is also possible that a person could participate in this community while retaining religious affiliation in an orthodox Christian community. In other words, while one need not hold any specific dogma or sacred text to be part of the community, one *could* certainly hold to specific dogmas and sacred texts *and* be a part of this community.

Pavlovitz describes himself as a "longtime Christian by aspiration (if not always in practice)."[62] And in the following passage he offers a provocative summary of his religious autobiography:

> My meandering, five-decade pilgrimage as a theological mutt—from obedient Catholic altar boy to disenchanted teen to hopeful agnostic to defiant atheist to overconfident United Methodist megachurch pastor to deconstructing

---

62 Pavlovitz, *If God is Love, Don't Be a Jerk*, 2.

progressive to humanist Christian to whoever and whatever I am today—hasn't yielded much in the way of definitive statements. In fact, the single conclusion I've come to as a result of all my study and prayer and wrestling and preaching, the sole fixed truth I can hold on to is that *faith shouldn't make you a jerk*. That's it.[63]

I suspect that statement would freak Childers out. But honestly, I don't know that what Pavlovitz says is that different from the Apostle Paul:

> If I speak in the tongues of men or of angels, but do not have love, I am only a resounding gong or a clanging cymbal. If I have the gift of prophecy and can fathom all mysteries and all knowledge, and if I have a faith that can move mountains, but do not have love, I am nothing. (1 Corinthians 13:1-2)

To sum up, the principle of charity requires me to conclude that Pavlovitz is indeed a Christian until I see some sufficient reason to deny his own confessional statement. And so, it seems to me that all five of our progressive Christians are indeed Christians, four are so without controversy and one with some outstanding question as to the nature of his identification with Unitarian Universalism.

What if the concerned evangelical is now thinking: "Okay, fair enough, maybe not *all* progressive Christians are fake Christians but what if *some* are?" My first response is: let's not lose sight of the fact that Childers offered no such qualification. She has brazenly slandered fellow brothers and sisters in Christ. Slander is defined as the making of false statements that damage a person's reputation. And claiming that genuine Christians are, in fact, malicious fakers, wolves, and tares certainly does that. At the very least, this reckless behavior calls into question her general reliability as a Christian leader and teacher.

---

63 Pavlovitz, *If God is Love, Don't Be a Jerk*, 57.

Having said that, let's return to the question posed by the concerned evangelical: what if not all self-described progressive Christians are orthodox Christians? We can answer that question by turning it back on our concerned evangelical: what if not all *evangelical* Christians are orthodox Christians? What if some of them have corrupted Christianity with their love of a particular political party? What if their allegiance to Jesus has been skewed by their devotion to a crass political populist whose name rhymes with "rump"? What if their penchant to wield their guns ever ready to "shoot a bad guy" while fear mongering about refugees fits poorly with Jesus' teaching on the sheep and goats in Matthew 25? What if they have on occasion confused Christianity with nationalism or a health and wealth gospel of capitalist prosperity?

Do you think there might be at least a few evangelicals who have made some of those serious errors? And if there are such folk, if there *might be*, perhaps the concerned evangelical should consider what that means for their own evangelical house before worrying about Christians in the progressive conversation. After all, we definitely would not want to make the mistake of straining theological gnats while swallowing camels or hyperfixating on specks in the eyes of other communities whilst missing the planks in our own.

A Conversation with Peter Enns

In the last section, I was seeking to rebut Childers' attacks on some of the specifics that comprise the group that she claims are fake Christians, tares sown by the devil into God's wheat, and conniving wolves out to slaughter sheep. It seems to me that the charges are beyond the pale. And a great way to make that point would be by hearing from one of these shadowy "progressive Christians" in their own words. Since I've known Peter Enns for several years, I emailed him, and we set up a time to talk. I have included a summary of our conversation below.

Given that Childers was denying that people like Enns are Christians at all, I thought it would make sense to begin by speaking about church identity. Enns shared that he has been attending an Episcopalian church for the last decade. Indeed, on the morning that I spoke with him he had just come from a men's breakfast at his church. Enns noted that he appreciates the liturgy: "I pray out of the Book of Common Prayer before class. I like the Episcopal communion." He added that he also appreciates the fact that Episcopalians "don't major in the things that drive evangelicalism," though he added that he made the shift "very deliberately and consciously, and not with a hatred toward evangelicalism." Interestingly, this story jibed closely with what I've read of Rachel Held Evans' journey to Episcopalianism.

When I asked Enns to share his thoughts on progressive Christianity, he stated that it is not a term he cares for or which he uses of himself: Enns prefers the terms 'innovative' and 'adaptive.' However, he acknowledged that there definitely are people who identify with the term, and he thought it might be fair to call it a movement. He added, "movements are hard to determine. All I know is that based on my Twitter feed and emails and Facebook and Instagram, it's a thing. I mean, people are coming out of a conservative point of view and saying, 'there's got to be something else.'" Enns added that in his view, "progressive Christianity is very similar to people who are using the word deconstruction."

Enns knew of Childers, so I asked him to share his thoughts on her brand of conservative evangelicalism. He observed that in his view it represents "a highly intellectualized iteration of Christianity. It's not intellectually compelling to many people, but it is an intellectual movement. And you have to go outside of that into a liturgical or mainline world to get something that maybe is more-full bodied." I agree with Enns here. The fact that Strobel and Childers both claim that doctrine is the foundation of Christianity attests, in my view, to the preoccupation of their tradition with right belief and cognitive assent.

This brings us to the binary mindset of evangelical and fundamentalist Christianity. As Enns plaintively observed, "It's the classic fallacy of, 'well, my tribe's, right, let me show you everybody else is wrong. And in fact, we're so right if you don't agree with this, you're not even Christian.'" (Sounds familiar, doesn't it?)

Next, Enns and I talked a bit about teaching and the struggles that some students have with deconstruction such as we saw in chapter 1 when reviewing Childers' own reaction to the progressive pastor. Enns recalled that he has taught many Christian students who were raised with a particular theologically and culturally narrow understanding of Christianity. When their understanding is challenged in the classroom, they often experience that disequilibrium of having long held assumptions challenged. But as Enns observed with respect to the professor's role in all this, "we didn't cause a faith crisis. They were set up for it." While the progressive pastor may have made some genuine missteps in leading the class, it seems to me this describes Childers as well: she was set up for an existential crisis not by the pastor but by her Christian upbringing.

I noted above that Enns prefers the preservationist/innovator terminology suggested by Brian McLaren to the term "progressive." These terms distinguish between Christians who seek to *preserve* a received set of doctrines and those who seek to innovate upon that received set in reflective engagement with the best knowledge of the present day. Enns reflected,

> I think I'm more of an innovator. But what I think is really nice about those terms is that they actually try to build some bridges between the groups, because people who are innovating are innovating for the purpose of preserving. They're not trying to throw away Christianity. Only if you're a fundamentalist do people think progressives are throwing away

Christianity. But you're trying to do what people have done since the biblical period, which is continually bring this past tradition into the present context. So innovators sort of preserve.

But people who preserve are normally very well aware of the fact that times change. And . . . we can't just repeat the first century. We can record the history of Christianity so they're aware that there is, let's say, 'updating' for lack of a better word . . . ."

So they're both emphasizing things that are worth keeping. But some of us are like, "Come on, guys, we can't keep saying the same stuff over and over again; you can't go back to the Westminster Standards of the 17th century and say this is the crowning achievement of Christianity."

And to be a pure preservationist, I think is a form of idolatry. Not to be too strong about that, but I think it's actually making something into your ultimate standard that's very historically conditioned. And I think that's a problem. And being purely innovation, what frustrates me . . . from some people who call themselves progressives, they don't really have a sense of the past.

There's a lot there but we can sum up Enns' thoughts in four key points.

First off, Enns begins with the assumption that everyone involved in this project of innovation and preservation is a Christian. Even though we may all make somewhat different judgments as to when to preserve and when to innovate, we share a common project with common goals.

Second, we should assume that everyone embarked on this project has good intentions and thus that that all are doing their best to bring Christianity faithfully into the present age; thus, we should refrain from questioning the motives of others, still less of attributing outright nefarious purposes to them or subjecting them to a summary heresy trial.

Third, Enns notes that each approach, however well-intentioned, nonetheless brings with it a risk. The preservationist could fall into the trap of idolatry by equating some past theological formulation with the Gospel itself. Meanwhile the innovationist can fall into the trap of failing to appreciate the wisdom of the past or the opportunity to learn from it.

Finally, this dynamic of preservation and adaptation is not a new thing but rather is and has always been part and parcel of the Christian journey: from the beginning, Christians have been seeking to faithfully present the Gospel in each age and that inevitably involves both preservation and adaptation.

McLaren's Liberal/Progressive vs. Erickson's Translator/Transformer

I think Enns is exactly right with his summary. Taken together, these four points provide a powerful critique of the simplistic binary mindset that undergirds Childers' attempts to otherize those whom she deems progressive and to fear-monger about them to those in her own tribe. Unfortunately, the binary mindset does not respond well to such nuanced views which undermine simple distinctions between insider and outsider in favor of a continuum of well-intentioned dialogue and debate. In this section, I want to unpack further the distinction between preservationists and innovationists by considering Brian McLarens' take on the liberal/progressive in contrast to conservative evangelical Millard Erickson's description of translators and transformers.

In his book *A Generous Orthodoxy* McLaren provides a memorable parable of these two contrasting approaches to theological reflection and adaptation. It appears in a chapter titled "I am a Liberal/Conservative," though the title could just as well have been "I am a progressive/evangelical Christian." And yes, the point is that McLaren is (and we all are) *both liberals and conservatives* because each of us finds ourselves innovating on some occasions and preserving on others. Given that this represents an ever-fluctuating continuum on the interface between Christian belief/practice and the world around us, you can't separate out two groups in any absolute manner, and certainly not in terms of Childers' binary opposition of heroes and villains.

But I'm getting ahead of myself. McLaren's parable tells the story of two groups travelling on a river by canoe. Both groups need to deliver some food and medicine to a plague-stricken village down river. But as they encounter obstacles like whitewater that increase the difficulty of passage, each canoe makes a different decision over how to continue. One canoe decides to toss some items overboard to adapt to the changing conditions of the river and then ride out the rapids. Meanwhile, the other canoe opts instead to pull out of the river altogether and portage over land with all their cargo intact.[64] The point is that there is no one right way to get down the river: each canoe wants to get as much of the cargo to the village and to do so in as short a time as possible, and each makes strategic decisions about what to give up (either objects in the canoe or the time it takes to get to the village) in order to achieve that common goal.

The main lessons include the following: first, every choice is a compromise; second, the choices are not exclusive, for we can all choose to pull out of the river at some points and remove items at other points and thus we're all liberals in some moments and conservatives in others; and third, the entire process is aimed at the end of getting the maximum amount of food and medicine to the village in as effective a means as possible. In other words, nobody is seeking to undermine the mission. Everyone has noble intentions, regardless of whether they make all the right decisions.

I really like that illustration. But it isn't perfect because it implies that the innovator who removes an item from the canoe

---

64 *A Generous Orthodoxy* (Zondervan, 2009), 141, ff.

is simply *subtracting* from the total commitment of belief. But the reality is more complicated . . . and far more interesting. The truth is that when one rejects a doctrine (i.e. removes an item) it is typically not merely a matter of *subtracting* an item but rather of *replacing* items. So if I were to add my own twist to the parable, I would switch from the idea of throwing items overboard to the scenario of innovative canoeists stopping at bartering stations on the riverbank and trading various items that have become too cumbersome for other items they believe to be better suited for the journey.

For a simple example of how this works, consider that for more than a thousand years, theologians wed the Christian theological system to a geocentric view of the universe rooted in a model developed by the second century astronomer and mathematician Ptolemy. According to that model, the earth is the fixed center of the universe and is surrounded by spheres that slowly turn around it with embedded celestial objects including the sun, moon, and stars. (Alas, comets never fit into the geocentric view since they stubbornly violated the boundaries of the spheres.) This ancient scientific model seemed to fit well with a Christian view of the universe, for it offered a clear place for hell and sheol (the place of the dead) within the bowels of the earth and it located heaven securely beyond the outermost celestial sphere. And so, when Jesus *ascended* to the right hand of the Father, he was literally *going up* and returning to God in heaven; and when he comes back, he will descend back to earth from that lofty abode.

Ptolemy's geocentric model of the universe fit very well within the canoe for a long time. But eventually, the canoe began to encounter rapids. They started off small with the proposal of an alternative, simpler model in which the sun was placed at the center (thanks, Copernicus). But the rapids grew significantly in 1610 when Galileo observed through his telescope four celestial objects orbiting around Jupiter. This discovery of the moons of Jupiter contradicted the geocentric model which claimed that all objects orbit around earth. From that point, the evidence quickly began to build for the theory resulting in some very daunting whitewater. Alas, not even imprisoning Galileo in 1633 could stem the tide of scientific advance. (Protip: jailing scientists tends not to work out well.) Gradually, Christian theologians were forced to face the fact that the geocentric model was becoming increasingly unwieldy. And one by one, they turned their canoes into the bartering station to exchange the geocentric model for a far more svelte Copernican model of the universe before returning to the river able to traverse the rapids.

That process has oft repeated itself as theology adapts to the ever-shifting horizons of scientific advance.[65] The story began replaying in the nineteenth century with the rise of an old earth model of geology and an evolutionary model of biology. Once again, theologians were challenged to make hard decisions about when to pull out of the river to trade an increasingly unwieldy scientific model (young earth catastrophism; special creation) for an updated model (old earth uniformitarianism; Neo-Darwinism). And of course, some folk (the young earth creationists) *never* stopped at the bartering station. Instead, they opted to pull out of the river and for the last century and a half they've been portaging overland with their young earth models of geology and special creationist biology intact.

The underlying flaw of Childers' binary thinking is illustrated well in another set of paired terms—translators and transformers—which comes from evangelical Baptist theologian Millard Erickson. In his popular textbook of conservative evangelical doctrine, *Christian Theology,* Erickson introduces these terms (borrowed from William Hordern) to refer to two different approaches to theology. He explains the difference as follows:

---

65 For an account of how science and theology relate to one another, see my book *Conversations with My Inner Atheist: A Christian Apologist Explores Questions that Keep People Up at Night* (2 Cup Press, 2020), chapter 9.

The translators are theologians who feel a need for reex-pressing the message in a more intelligible form, but intend to retain the content, as one does when translating from one language to another. The transformers, however, as the name would indicate, are prepared to make rather serious changes in the content of the message in order to relate it to the modern world.[66]

Unfortunately, the way Erickson contrasts these two groups is deeply skewed by the binary mindset. On his account, trans-lators have good intentions to "retain the content" but trans-formers intend, rather, to "make serious changes." While he doesn't quite say it, the implication is clear: transformers have a corrupt intention to distort the meaning of Christianity. In this manner, Erickson impugns the motives of the (transforming liberal) outgroup. The implication is that evangelical Christians are faithful translators while liberal Christians are malicious transformers. Childers' framework is pretty much the same except that she instead targets malicious progressives.

The great strength of the Enns/McLaren framework is that it deconstructs this simplistic binary mindset between good guys with good intentions who faithfully translate and bad guys with bad intentions who maliciously transform. Instead, it recognizes that we are all on the river and we all need to make decisions at various points about what to retain (even if it requires a laborious portage) and what to toss or trade.

Erickson's binary mindset inhibits one's ability either to see the insights in the other or the weakness in one's own theological perspective. While I think there is some value in Erickson's contrast, that value goes only insofar as we recognize that *we all aim to translate*. As Enns put it, "Translation is the history of Christian thought and biblical thought." And as for the other side of the coin, *we are all in danger of transforming*. The conservative can fall into this trap as surely as anyone

---

66 *Christian Theology*, 2nd ed. (Baker, 1998), 123.

else: after all, a conservative exists as such with respect to a tradition that he/she maintains and *tradition is not infallible*.

For a particularly egregious example, consider that in the early 1960s many churches in the United States were opposed to the Civil Rights movement and the call for the racial integration of churches. Within the context of the Deep South in this period, the racially segregated Baptist church seeking to defend "the way we've always done it" was the conservative seeking to preserve a traditional stance. However, that traditional stance was morally flawed, indeed demonic. By contrast, the innovators were doing nothing more than calling out that evil and challenging those churches to discover what it actually means to be one in Christ Jesus as in Galatians 3:28. In that case, which church do you think was in danger of transforming the Gospel? (Spoiler alert: it wasn't the progressive innovators.)

To sum up, pursuing the goal of translation by way of the twin efforts of preservation and innovation, that's just what it is to be a thinking Christian. It is a task in which we are all engaged. Adopting a binary mindset that impugns the motives and dismisses the efforts of an outgroup simply because we disagree with some of their choices effectively blinds us to the insights they may have for us as well as the potential blind spots and weaknesses in our own efforts.

How Childers Misrepresents Progressive Christianity

To conclude this chapter, I want to address one final and very serious way that Childers misrepresents the nature of progressive Christianity. Childers points out that progressive Christians take the view that affiliation with that movement entails a commitment to conversation but not to any specific doctrine. Fair enough, but then Childers appears to conclude that the individuals who participate in the conversation are thereby themselves not committed to any doctrine. As an analysis of progressive Christianity, that is either fundamentally confused or deeply disingenuous for *one can have deep personal theolog-ical convictions* while *participating in a conversation that does not require any specific deep personal theological convictions* from the participants. Thus, the fact that an individual par-ticipates in the conversation tells you *precisely nothing* about their personal commitments beyond the fact that they're open to conversation with others.

To illustrate, any individual can sign up to take one of my systematic theology courses. The seminary does not require a specific confession of faith from individual participants in order to take a course. But that fact does not thereby imply that all those who take my theological courses have no per-sonal theological commitments. By the same token, a person can participate in an open "progressive" conversation that has no overarching creed or statement of belief while personally confessing a specific creed and a robust statement of belief. That's the quick overview of how Childers distorts the pro-gressive conversation. Now let's consider in more detail how she presents this fallacy.

Repeatedly, Childers insists that progressive Christianity lacks any cohesive set of underlying beliefs or practices or unifying creedal commitments. She makes the point by citing theologian F. LeRon Shults to that effect. (In fact, Shults is actually describing the emergent movement of the early 2000s but Childers takes that movement to be the forerunner of today's progressive Christianity.) According to Shults, emer-gent doesn't have a statement of faith because that "tends to stop conversation . . . ."[67] Childers then moves from the trivial fact that the *conversation* does not require participants to assent to some set of doctrines to the erroneous conclusion that individuals who participate in the conversation thereby don't assent to any doctrines: "Progressive Christians tend to avoid absolutes and are typically not united around creeds or belief

---

67 Childers, *Another Gospel?* 73.

statements."[68] The reasoning seems to be that since progressive Christianity lacks any unifying doctrine and given that it is characterized rather by a willingness to question, that those who participate in the conversation thereby lack commitment to doctrines. As she puts it, progressive Christianity represents a "hodgepodge of beliefs."[69] Beyond that "hodgepodge," the only thing uniting progressive Christians is "a willingness to question the things historic Christians had believed and put their hope in for two thousand years."[70]

When you put it that way, it certainly *sounds* ominous, doesn't it? However, that is a good description of my seminary theology classroom as well. My students are not "united around creeds or belief statements." To be sure, I would suspect that most (if not all) of my students in any given semester would affirm basic ecumenical statements like the Apostles' and Nicene creeds. The point, however, is that adherence to such creeds is not a *requirement* for participation in the classroom experience. Yes, to some degree that results in a "hodgepodge of beliefs" if by "hodgepodge" we just mean *diversity*. But that's what happens when you talk to people who don't share all your opinions: you create a community with *diverse opinions*. Does that sound scary? It shouldn't.

Childers' choice of the word "hodgepodge" to refer to the progressive community is clearly intended to signal not just *diversity* but *lack of coherent integration*. However, that is a gross misrepresentation since there is no need for all participants to integrate their beliefs with one another into some sort of group mind or shared creed: the point is that there *isn't* a creedal restriction on discussion. Thus, it is utterly misleading to describe the diversity that exists among conversational participants as a "hodgepodge." The real value of diversity is that we all learn from one another as iron sharpens iron.

---

68 Childers, *Another Gospel?* 8.

69 Childers, *Another Gospel?* 76.

70 Childers, *Another Gospel?* 76.

And I assure you that my Pentecostal students and Reformed students and Baptist students and Methodist students and Catholic students (yes, I have a few of those) always challenge one another with their very different perspectives on an endless array of theological subjects.

Every year in my two main sequence systematic theology classes, I have students write a personal doctrinal statement summarizing their views of a range of topics: the first semester includes prolegomena, doctrine of God, doctrine of creation, doctrine of the fall; the second semester includes doctrine of Christ and salvation, doctrine of the Holy Spirit and the church, and doctrine of last things. At the end, each student has written a robust personal statement of approximately twenty pages outlining their theological convictions and remaining questions. I assure you that the personal statements of belief that my students produce are very far from a "hodgepodge." And that's the level at which integration matters.

Over the years, most of my students have produced statements on a broad spectrum from fundamentalist and conservative Protestant to progressive and liberal Protestant. As I said, I also have the occasional Roman Catholic and a smattering of other outliers: for example, I once had a student who was Oneness Pentecostal (a denomination that rejects the doctrine of the Trinity), another who was a Messianic Jew, and another who rejected the historic resurrection of Jesus. Time and again, I emphasize to my students that my task is not to grade their orthodoxy: that will happen soon enough when they seek ministry opportunities in various church communities! Rather, my task is to grade their ability to articulate their beliefs and understand where those beliefs stand relative to historic orthodox standards.

That's how you should think of progressive Christianity, especially for those who don't have the luxury of joining a graduate theological community. All are welcome to that conversation just like all are welcome to the seminary theology classroom. The conversation is constituted by a diversity of perspectives (call it a hodgepodge if you like). And within that exciting welter of diversity, we are all invited to share our own personal convictions and questions without fear of censure or stigma as together we reflect on what it means to be a Christian in the twenty-first century.

Just as my theology classroom has a diversity of perspectives, so our brief survey of five individuals Childers calls progressive reveals significant diversity ranging from Rohr's mystical Catholicism to Zahnd's small 'o' orthodoxy to Enns and Evans' Episcopalianism. As for Pavlovitz, what if he is ultimately a Unitarian Universalist who has set aside multiple historic orthodox doctrines? I'll tell you this: based on the thought-provoking nature of his writings, he would be a great contributor in any seminary classroom, and I have no doubt that other students would be challenged by his perspective. I definitely appreciate his emphasis on the primacy of love of people (especially in contrast to the evangelical love of culture wars). Needless to say, you don't have to agree with people to have a good conversation with them or to learn from them!

As I noted above, Zahnd replied to Childers' claim that he is a progressive Christian (but not a real one) with the quote "When you label me, you negate me." The sad truth is that Alisa Childers has chosen to label and thereby negate many fellow Christians. In addition, she misleadingly construes an ongoing open conversation of theological reflection as if it is somehow equivalent to a new religious sect in which all participants reject specific doctrines in favor of a hodgepodge of discordant convictions. But as we have seen, this is a profoundly misleading characterization. Progressive Christianity is, as Enns noted, just part of what it is to be Christian participating in an ongoing process of questioning and theological reflection as each of us considers anew what it means to be Christian in our day.

4

Humility about Knowledge
is Not Relativism about Truth

Time and again, I find a common error among many conservative Christians: they confuse a healthy awareness of our own fallibility in knowledge with relativism about truth. For example, they encounter statements like "All our truth claims are subject to error" and they conclude from this that the individual who made the statement *doesn't care about truth* or that they *adopt relativism about truth*. But that doesn't follow at all. Such statements simply constitute a perfectly defensible recognition of epistemic humility that acknowledges our weaknesses and limitations in *grasping* truth. As we will see in this chapter, Childers commits this basic category error in *Another Gospel?*

At the outset, I freely admit there may be self-described progressive Christians who do adopt relativism about truth. Just as I cannot opine definitively on the personal convictions of every student who takes my theology courses in a given semester, so I certainly cannot opine on the personal convictions of every individual who may identify with the wider progressive Christian conversation. But remember, there also may be evangelicals who think Donald Trump is a prophet of God. That doesn't mean we should assume those opinions are shared by the entire evangelical community.

What I *can* do is point out how specific examples that Childers provides as alleged evidence for relativism about truth are, in fact, better interpreted as a perfectly reasonable *epistemic humility* regarding our ability to grasp truth. Additionally, I can also point to evidence that the very people that Childers alleges reject objective truth actually affirm it. This evidence will be sufficient to undermine the reliability of Childers' analysis on this topic.

While epistemic humility can seem to those of a binary mindset like a direct assault on truth itself, this misreading arises from the individual's own failure to recognize their limitations . . . or to appreciate the strengths in the perspectives of others. The truth is that epistemic humility is not only *consistent* with Christian conviction, but passages like 1 Corinthians 13:12 suggest that it is *implied* by mature Christian faith underscored by our own intrinsic finitude and the fallenness that skews our perspective.[71]

Truth, Relativism, Confusion

Conservative evangelical Christians talk a lot about the importance of objective truth and they have a long history of galvanizing support for Christian ministries, selling Christian books, and promoting lectures and courses by fear mongering about the rising specter of relativism about truth.[72] Thus,

---

71 On the latter point, theologians refer to the "noetic effects of sin," and how it impacts our ability to reason. For an analysis of our ability to self-deceive (which is one key aspect of those noetic effects) see Gregg A. Ten Elshof, *I Told Me So: Self-Deception and the Christian Life* (Eerdmans 2009).

72 For further discussion of the concept of truth and its rhetorical role in conservative evangelicalism, see Rauser, *You're Not as Crazy as I Think*, chapter 2. Also see Randal Rauser, "Learning in a Time of (Cultural) War:

when Childers repeatedly warns that progressive Christians are relativists, she is tapping into some timeworn strategies for building a profile to this conservative evangelical constituency, one that invokes a reliable bogeyman to galvanize opposition to a common enemy.[73]

Before we wade any further into that dubious approach to ministry-building, we should say a few words about the nature of truth itself. The core idea of truth involves a *matching relationship* between reality and our beliefs or statements about it, a relationship that is most frequently described in terms of *correspondence*.[74] For example, the statement "It is sunny today" is true if and only if that statement corresponds to reality, that is, only if it really is sunny today. By the same token, "Jesus rose from the dead" is true if and only if that statement corresponds to reality such that Jesus really did rise from the dead. The core idea is that truth in its nature is *objective* and thus something that we discover.

We also need to recognize, however, that one can affirm an objective correspondence theory of truth while also adopting a *relative view* of that correspondence in particular domains. For example, the statement "The soup is chicken noodle" is wholly objective and finds its truth conditions solely in the objective fact of what kind of soup it is. But "The soup is delicious" is a case where the truth-making fact to which the statement would correspond is the mental disposition of an individual. And depending on what particular individuals think, the statement could be true *and* false. Thus, the soup either is chicken noodle or it isn't, but relative to Smith the

---

Indoctrination in Focus on the Family's 'The Truth Project,'™'" *Christian Scholars' Review,* vol. 39, no. 1 (2009), 75-89.

73 I'm not claiming that she does not believe the claims she makes, for one can employ an effective strategy whilst believing in the truth-claims associated with it.

74 There are other theories of truth as well, though I will not consider them here. For a very good philosophical introduction see Richard Kirkham, *Theories of Truth: A Critical Introduction* (Bradford, 1995).

soup may be delicious while relative to Jones it may be insipid. This is still a correspondence view of truth, but in the case of taste the correspondence is to subjective facts constituted by the relative opinions of individuals.[75]

I'm going to assume that Childers would concede that a realist correspondence theory of truth can allow for a subset of statements in which the truth of the claim is fixed, at least in part, relative to the subjective beliefs of specific individuals. This would still allow us to say that in a vast range of other cases from the sunniness of the day to the emptiness of Jesus' tomb, that the truthfulness of the statements is fixed by correspondence to objective facts about the world alone.

Childers' comments on truth are inextricably linked to her comments about knowledge so we'll begin there even though we're going to cycle back to knowledge again later. She writes that critics of an objective view of truth had "a belief that the church was much too influenced by modernism (the idea that truth could be found through common sense, logic, human reason, and science) . . . ."[76] In Childers' view, these critics are linked with "postmodernism" which "rejects the idea that absolute truth can be known."[77] Note that in these statements Childers is not simply addressing the nature of truth itself but rather the epistemological question of *whether truth can be known*. Indeed, in the second quote she uses the term "*absolute truth*" which muddies the waters because the term is ambiguous between *objective* truth (a metaphysical or reality claim)

---

75 One can accept this basic correspondence account of truth while also recognizing that some statements may lack clear truth conditions because they are ambiguous or because they are vague. An example of an ambiguous statement is "Larry the cannibal had his neighbor for dinner": given that it is not clear whether Larry *ate* his neighbor or *ate with* his neighbor, the truth conditions of the statement remain unclear. An example of a statement with vague truth conditions is "Larry is bald" because baldness is itself a vague concept (it isn't clear how much hair one must lack before qualifying as bald) and thus it might not be clear when Larry would qualify as bald thereby making the statement true.

76 Childers, *Another Gospel?* 71.

77 Childers, *Another Gospel?* 72.

and an *absolute or certain grasp* of truth (an epistemological
or knowledge claim).

Childers then contrasts "absolute truth" or simply "the
truth" with the concept of relative truth or "my truth."[78] She
illustrates the difference with bacon. As Childers puts it, if you
Google the word "bacon", you will encounter a mixture of truth
claims, some of which are "facts" (i.e. they correspond to the
nature of bacon) and others which are "fantasy" (i.e. they do
not correspond to the nature of bacon). We do not have the
luxury of *choosing* which claim is true just because we like it.
This is how she puts it: "If 'my truth' says pork is the new kale,
the consequences of that idea will bear out in reality—despite
how strongly I may feel about it. My feelings about bacon won't
change what it's doing to my heart, my blood pressure, and
my thighs. This is why 'my truth' is a myth."[79]

The message is clear. Childers is claiming that progressive
Christians widely accept these relativistic notions of truth,
notions in which they claim that objective truth cannot be
known, and they instead define truth in terms of the subjective whim of the individual: if I want to *believe* that bacon is
healthy then bacon *is* healthy! If I want to believe there is no
hell, then there is no hell! Easy peasy! But Childers insists that
responding to the skeptical dilemma by redefining the nature
of truth as wholly relative to the individual is disastrous: "We
can't allow truth to be sacrificed on the altar of our feelings."[80]

Is there good evidence that this is, in fact, how progressive
Christians think about truth? Are they really tossing out the
concept of objective (correspondence) truth altogether in favor
of a subjective notion where the individual can manufacture
facts about the nutritional status of foodstuffs at will? Again,
it is always possible that there are folk in the progressive conversation who believe they can invent facts at will. But if such

---

78 Childers, *Another Gospel?* 10-11.

79 Childers, *Another Gospel?* 11.

80 Childers, *Another Gospel?* 11.

people exist, I suspect they are a rare commodity indeed. After all, the brute facticity of objective existence has a way of disappointing our expectations and frustrating our desires. It seems to me that going forward, the best way to evaluate Childers' claim is by considering whether this kind of radical relativism is present in the leaders that she targets. So let's turn to some examples.

I'll start with a recent article on Pavlovitz's blog titled "No, All Opinions are Not Equally Valid."[81] The article was prompted by Pavlovitz's interaction with a man who was defending FOX News host Tucker Carlson's reporting on the Russian war with Ukraine. Pavlovitz replies: "One of the greatest lies people propagate is that all opinions are valid: that every position is somehow equally worthy of merit and deserving of consideration."[82] On the contrary, Pavlovitz stresses that not all opinions are equally valid and it is the *objective facts* of the matter that determine the truthfulness and value of what you say. To circle back to FOX News, Tucker Carlson *can't just make stuff up and call it news*.

If we turn to Pavlovitz's most recent book *If God is Love, Don't be a Jerk* we find him defending the thesis that legitimate religion should make you kinder and more loving: as Pavlovitz puts it, "the sole fixed truth I can hold on to, is that *faith shouldn't make you a jerk*."[83] The whole point is that this thesis is not true just because Pavlovitz wills it so. Rather, this is a *fixed truth*, one that he has *discovered*.

Peter Enns likewise is committed to objective truth. In his youth curriculum *Telling God's Story* he explains in the introduction why the course begins with Jesus rather than the Old Testament: "We are beginning at the culmination of the story,

---

81 Pavlovitz, "No, All Opinions are Not Equally Valid," *Stuff that Needs to Be Said* (March 18, 2022), https://johnpavlovitz.com/2022/03/18/no-all-opinions-are-not-equally-valid/

82 Pavlovitz, "No, All Opinions are Not Equally Valid."

83 Pavlovitz, *If God is Love, Don't be a Jerk*, 57.

to see how all of this ends up—acquainting children with the *most central truths* of the Scripture before we go back to fill in the many interesting details."[84] "The truths of the Scripture" are not made true by the subjective whim of Peter Enns (or any other reader) but rather by their correspondence to an objective reality. This is hammered home in lesson 17 of the curriculum which addresses the question of character under the directive "Just Be Truthful."[85]

Enns also clearly assumes an objective understanding of truth when discussing the discipline of history in his book *Inspiration and Incarnation*: "All written accounts of history are *literary products* that are based on *historical events* that are shaped to conform to the *purpose* the historian wants to get across."[86] While the historian always has an interest and perspective in telling history, that which is told is ostensibly based on and thus corresponds to actual *historical events*. The truthfulness of the historical account depends not on the whims of the historian or the reader but rather on the accuracy with which the historian's account relays those past events.

I could keep going through our other progressive thought leaders citing similar examples. But I don't want to belabor the point. To be blunt, it is simply *absurd* to claim that a radical relativism in which truth is manufactured by personal whim is an opinion seriously defended by leading progressive Christians. And once again, there could always be outliers in this dizzyingly vast conversation that hold such views just like there can be idiosyncratic views in my theology classroom . . . or in your local evangelical church. But it is indeed absurd to suggest that such views are somehow common. If such attitudes exist at all, I suspect they are rare as hen's teeth. Thus, to claim this

---

84 Enns, *Telling God's Story. Year One: Meeting Jesus* (Olive Branch Books, 2010), 7, emphasis added.

85 Enns, *Telling God's Story*, 54, ff.

86 Enns, *Inspiration and Incarnation: Evangelicals and the Problem of the Old Testament*, 2nd ed. (Baker Academic, 2015), 62.

kind of relativism is a representative view in the progressive conversation is a clear strawman.

Rob Bell, Relativist?

Having just declared Childers' take a strawman, I want to add that I'm not quite done with the relativism charge. In this section, we will consider the most prominent alleged example of relativism that Childers gives us. Analyzing her example will illustrate definitively how the thesis fails as well as how the actual issue at play concerns not *relativism about truth* but rather *epistemic humility as regards our grasp of truth.*

That most notable example of alleged relativism about truth that Childers provides comes in her chapter on "Authority Problems" when she sets her sights on Rob Bell. She begins by citing an excerpt from Bell's book *What is the Bible? How an Ancient Library of Poems, Letters, and Stories Can Transform the Way You Think and Feel About Everything.* Here is the excerpt:

> They were taught by their pastor or parents or authority figures to submit to the authority of the Bible, but *that's impossible to do without submitting first to whoever is deciding what the Bible is even saying . . . .* The problem, of course, is that the folks who talk the most about the authority of the Bible also seem to talk the most about things like objective and absolute truth, truth that exists *independent of relational realities.*[87]

After quoting this passage, Childers refers back to her bacon example from earlier in the book: just because you *want* bacon to be healthier than kale doesn't make it so because truth is not *created by our desires* but rather *discovered by our engagement with objective reality.*[88] Needless to say, the implication is

87 Cited in Childers, *Another Gospel?* 161.

88 Childers, *Another Gospel?* 10-11.

that Childers interprets Bell's apparently dismissive comment regarding "objective and absolute truth" as implying that he accepts that we just *create truth based on our desires*. If you *want* bacon to be healthier than kale, then you can just make it so.

I agree that this Bell quote might seem at first blush to fit Childers' narrative. So you might be thinking, perhaps this is that rare as hen's teeth instance of a progressive Christian who actually embraces a radically subjective notion of truth as something we merely create by an act of will. While conceding an anomaly here wouldn't undermine my main point that such views are not representative of the progressive conversation, the fact remains that this is *not* what Bell is saying at all. Nor could any honest reader who carefully considers what Bell says conclude that such a reading is remotely plausible.

You don't need to stray far from this passage in Bell's text to understand what he is *actually* saying. On the previous page he sets up the point by asserting that "the Bible has to be interpreted."[89] That is the overarching point he is making. He goes on to explain that we read the Bible differently because we all grant authority to specific perspectives in our interpretation of the text. None of us comes to the biblical text from a neutral, unmediated perspective. Thus, when Bell refers negatively to "objective and absolute truth, truth that exists *independent of relational realities*," he is not denying the claim that truth is independent of our desire or will; rather, he is denying that we ever *access* truth apart from our limited perspective. In short, he is pointing out that finite human beings do not occupy what philosophers call a *God's eye point of view* or a *view from nowhere* in which we can just see things as they are.[90]

---

89 Bell, *What is the Bible? How an Ancient Library of Poems, Letters, and Stories Can Transform the Way You Think and Feel About Everything* (Harper-One, 2017), 270.

90 For a famous philosophical treatment of this question, see Thomas Nagel, *The View From Nowhere* (Oxford University Press, 1989).

Rather, our engagement with reality is always from a limited point of view: that is, it is necessarily *perspectival*. And this, in turn, entails that we always read the Bible from a point of view or finite perspective.

There's a simple illustration of the point Bell is making. It starts with the old fundamentalist bumper sticker:

God said it. I believe it. That settles it.

The problem with this popular slogan is that it removes the role of interpretation from the equation: that is, it fails to recognize the role that *reading* and thus *interpreting* that which was said plays in the transmission of a message. Instead, the slogan seems to assume that one can simply imbibe a message directly.

This is a woefully misguided notion for texts are always interpreted, and that includes the Bible. If we are to appreciate the dynamics of how we get at the truth contained within the Bible, a truth that always comes to us from a point of view, we need to add a step. That step begins with a recognition that we are *reading* the text:

God said it. *I read it.* I believe it. That settles it.

This added step might seem to be so trivial as not to be worth mentioning. But sometimes the obvious needs to be high-lighted. In fact, once we recognize that to get at textual truth we need to read and thus to *interpret,* we can begin to capture the "relational realities" to which Bell refers.

A lot is actually packed into the act of reading itself which further illustrates the importance of recognizing relational realities. Some years ago, I saw the following slogan on a T-shirt which unpacks in admirable detail some of the essential dimensions to that process of reading and thus *interpreting* a text. Here it is:

God said it.

I interpreted it
As best I could in light of all the filters imposed
by my upbringing and culture,
which I try to control for
but you can never do a perfect job.

That doesn't exactly settle it,
But it does give me enough of a platform
to base my values and decisions on.

What this revised slogan loses in concision it more than makes up for in accuracy. Note first that there is not a hint of relativism about truth in this revised maxim just as there isn't in Bell's analysis. The claim isn't that we *invent* truth on a subjective whim akin to Childers' bacon lover conjuring up nutritional facts.

Rather, the overarching themes here are two. This expanded maxim represents *perspectivism*, the understanding that there is no God's eye point of view, and thus, as Bell said, no access to truth independent of relational realities. The second point it reflects is *fallibilism*, the view that given how our engagement with reality is always limited it is prone to error and should remain open to correction and revision as required.

Some years ago, Lesslie Newbigin wrote a very helpful little book discussing these themes called *Proper Confidence*. It is essentially a book-length unpacking of the themes of our much-expanded bumper sticker maxim culminating in the observation that while matters are not settled (i.e. we could always be wrong about the truth) we nonetheless have a sufficient basis to form beliefs and move forward in the world. And that's what Newbigin helpfully labels as "proper confidence."[91]

---

91 *Proper Confidence: Faith, Doubt, and Certainty in Christian Discipleship* (Eerdmans, 1995).

In none of this do we find the idea that truth is something we manufacture on a whim. Bell is *not* endorsing a subjective, relativistic view of truth at all. Rather, he is articulating the importance of epistemic humility, especially as we engage the biblical text and work out our own theology.

Rob Bell on Truth

It isn't simply that Childers falsely interprets a particular passage in Bell's book as relativist. It is also the case that she ignores the multiple places in his book where Bell offers robust objectivist language about truth. For example, he states that the phrase "God's truth" is redundant because "If it's true, then it's from God." In other words, truth isn't fixed by our subjective whim but rather by God's providential action. Bell then adds that he draws this point from medieval theologian Thomas Aquinas and modern Reformed philosopher Arthur Holmes,[92] both of whom famously endorsed a thoroughly objective and realist understanding of truth as something we *discover* rather than something we *create*.

Next, Bell describes people *stumbling upon* the truth and he notes, "Faith is about embracing truth wherever it's found, and that of course includes science."[93] The point is that you stumble upon and thus find things that exist objectively out there. This is not the language of personal whim creation. Bell then states that when Paul was writing to the Corinthians, he was seeking to make them "the kind of people who embrace the truth wherever they *find* it."[94] Thus, once again we find Bell appealing to the objective language of truth as *discovery* of that which is outside oneself. The entire framework of Bell's comments *assumes* that truth is something objective that we

---

92 Bell, *What is the Bible?* 175.

93 Bell, *What is the Bible?* 175.

94 Bell, *What is the Bible?* 175.

discover in the world. It is something we *find,* not something we create.

At the risk of belaboring the point, I'm going to provide three more examples from Bell's book. First example: on page 77, Bell writes: "We started with the very straightforward truth that the Bible was written by real people living in real places at real times."[95] Here are two possible ways to take Bell's claim:

- *Objectivist Interpretation:* the statement "the Bible was written by real people living in real places at real times" is made true by the fact that the Bible was written by real people living in real places at real times.
- *Relativist Interpretation:* the statement "the Bible was written by real people living in real places at real times" is made true by the fact that Bell wants it to be true (analogous to Childers' example of wanting bacon to be healthy).

Honestly, how could anyone think that Childers' relativist interpretation is a serious contender here?

Now for our second example. Bell writes the following on page 167: "You refer to yourself as the logical, rational type who doesn't go for fairy tales. But the truth is, you've had experiences that don't fit into any of your nice, neat, modern categories."[96] If we needed one more knockdown refutation of Childers' accusation, this is certainly it. Reality *often* challenges us by foiling our expectations. The truth about reality is thus not a product of our subjective desires but rather cold hard facts we run into . . . whether we want to or not!

Our final example offers a deliciously ironic smackdown of Childers' bacon example. On page 165, Bell reflects on the Apostle Peter's revelation about how God has made unclean foods clean by asking: "How did God show Peter this new

---

95 Bell, *What is the Bible?* 77.

96 Bell, *What is the Bible?* 167.

truth?"[97] Does that question sound like it assumes truth by way of relativist creation-by-subjective-desire? Far from it! Contrary to Childers' bacon example, the very *last* thing Peter wanted was to eat bacon! Nonetheless, God spoke to him, revealing the objective truth that bacon is now permissible to eat (even if it is still not healthy) and frustrating his expectations and opposition to the food in the process. Bell's text could not be clearer that truth is a matter of discovery rather than a willy-nilly creation of our relative desires.

To sum up, it is simply *stunning* to me that Childers can claim Bell is invoking a radical relativist notion of truth as something we *create* by fiat through the exercise of our fleeting subjective will as in the person who *wants* bacon to be "healthy" and thereby wills it so. Not only is that an obvious misreading of the text Childers quotes in which Bell is actually critiquing the fabled God's eye point of view, but throughout the rest of the book Bell consistently speaks about truth as an objective reality we discover rather than something we create. Ironically, the best hope for Childers to make her analysis true is by adopting a relativistic notion of truth so that she can simply will it be so!

Objective Truth and the Progressive Conversation

In the previous chapter we considered how Childers misrepresents progressive Christianity as a clearly defined movement that lacks a creedal center. On the contrary, it is more like an open classroom where students come together in a common interest to ask questions and pursue theological understanding. While Childers says ominously that progressives "tend to avoid absolutes" and thus objective truth, as we have seen the matter is quite otherwise. Indeed, the understanding of truth as something we *pursue* and *discover* undergirds the entire progressive conversation.

---

97 Bell, *What is the Bible?*, 165.

Right after Childers warns that progressives allegedly avoid absolutes, she turns a critical eye to an essay by John Pavlovitz, in which he opines that there are "no sacred cows" for progressives.[98] No absolutes? No sacred cows? Once again, it sounds ominous at first blush, doesn't it? Heck, it might even seem to confirm Childers' warning about relativism!

And once again, a closer look reveals something very different. Let's start with definitions. The term "sacred cow" refers to any entity (e.g. an organization, practice, object, or belief) which is considered exempt from any possible criticism or questioning. Thus, when you say there are no sacred cows, you are saying there are no organizations, practices, objects, or beliefs which are considered exempt from possible criticism or questioning.

Now why would someone *do* that? Why would they subject *everything* to questioning? Is it because they deny the existence of objective truth altogether? Is it because they believe that truth is just something we create on a whim? Perhaps, although in that case, why worry about questioning at all? Just *make true* whatever you want to be true! Surely there is a far simpler and more plausible explanation. Once you recognize that we don't have access to a God's eye point-of-view and thus that all human knowledge arises from a specific *perspective* (perspectivism) and represents a *fallible* grasp of reality (fallibilism), you must consider that for any organization you are a part of, any practice you undertake, any object you value, or any belief you hold, that it could be in error to some degree. In other words, it may fail to *match up to reality* and thus to be objectively true, good, or beneficial. The whole point of questioning everything is that you could be wrong in your pursuit of truth.

If you want an outstanding example of people who were committed to this bold principle, consider the Bereans. When Paul came to their synagogue, he set his sights on some deeply

---

98 Cited in Childers, *Another Gospel?* 8.

held beliefs about the messiah. Indeed, if you want a sacred cow in first century Judaism, consider the doctrine that messiah would be a military conqueror who would liberate the Jews from the yoke of the Romans. Paul challenged the Bereans to reconsider these deeply held beliefs in the light of new evidence. He was asking them to reconsider a doctrinal sacred cow about the messiah. When Paul had attempted the same thing earlier in the synagogue of Thessalonica things had not gone well. It turns out that for the Thessalonians, there are some doctrines you cannot question. But "the Berean Jews were of more noble character than those in Thessalonica, for they received the message with great eagerness and examined the Scriptures every day to see if what Paul said was true." (Acts 17:11) That's what it means to have no sacred cows. It's not about being irreverent or against God and it certainly isn't about dismissing objective truth. On the contrary, it is about the relentless and bold *pursuit* of truth seasoned with a healthy recognition of our own limitations and the endless capacity of reality to surprise.

When Pavlovitz says that there are sacred cows for the progressive Christian, what he's saying is that the Christian must always be ready to update their current beliefs based on new evidence in a relentless pursuit of the truth. Here is the full quote from the essay:

> There are no sacred cows, only the relentless, sacred search for Truth. Tradition, dogma, and doctrine are all fair game, because all pass through the hands of flawed humanity, and as such are all equally vulnerable to the prejudices, fears, and biases of those it touched.[99]

Pavlovitz's statement is not a rejection of absolute truth. On the

---

99 Pavlovitz, "Progressive Christianity—is Christianity," *Stuff that Needs to be Said* (October 5, 2016), https://johnpavlovitz.com/2016/10/05/explaining-progressive-christianity-otherwise-known-as-christianity/

contrary, it reflects an abiding commitment to pursue objective truth, a desire to understand things as they are, seasoned with a healthy recognition of our own limitations and proneness to error. As Paul said, "For now we see only a reflection as in a mirror; then we shall see face to face. Now I know in part; then I shall know fully, even as I am fully known." (1 Corinthians 13:12) Yes, we do see, but for now we see only as in a mirror.

Interestingly, Childers quotes the full passage from Pavlovitz later at the beginning of chapter 5,[100] though she still seems not to *understand* what she is quoting because she uses the passage to frame a discussion alleging that progressive Christians lack an objective doctrinal foundation. As we have seen, however, Pavlovitz's quote actually fits comfortably with a commitment to pursuing truth seasoned with epistemic humility. The Bereans didn't *lack* doctrine; rather, the point is that they were willing to *question their understanding* of doctrine in the light of new evidence.

Progressive Christianity just is Christianity

Pavlovitz begins his article with a quote from a friend: "Progressive Christianity is just Christianity. We are Christians—and we are progressing in our knowledge and understanding."[101] In our conversation, Enns said something similar when he observed that Christians who innovate in response to doctrinal challenges are simply "trying to do what people have done since the biblical period, which is continually bring this past tradition into the present context." So it isn't just a bit of rhetoric to say that progressive Christianity just is Christianity. It really is true.

If there is any distinctive to those in the progressive conversation, it might be that they are more aware of their own epistemic limitations and fallibility in the process than some other

---

100 Childers, *Another Gospel?* 71.

101 Pavlovitz, "Progressive Christianity—is Christianity."

Christians have been. And as a result, they would be more open to rethinking their doctrine as new evidence emerges . . . just like the Bereans.

It's also worth pointing out that this picture fits well with the Protestant Reformation description of the Christian Church as *ecclesia semper reformanda est,* the Church as *always reforming.* And that which is true of the Church generally is also true of her individual members: each of us should always be reforming, always questioning, always reflecting, and always and ever seeking to grow in our understanding of truth.

To conclude, I'd like to say a word about seeking truth and discerning error beyond the binary mindset. Some years ago, I wrote a companion book to William Paul Young's *The Shack* titled *Finding God in the Shack.*[102] At the time, I was interviewed multiple times about the controversies surrounding Young's book. On several occasions, I heard people warn against reading the book with the following ominous illustration: "if a cake batter had just a teaspoon of poop in it, would you eat the cake? Certainly not! Even a small amount of poop can ruin a cake. And even a seemingly small theological error can ruin a person's whole theology. So, if there are even seemingly small theological errors in *The Shack* you should toss the whole book."

That sounds like an illustration that Alisa Childers would use. If there is an error in progressive Christianity (meaning an error in some individual who identifies as a progressive Christian), then that error infects the whole and so we ought to toss it all out. So, if even a few progressives are mistaken about the nature of truth or some other matter, we still ought to shut down the whole conversation as contaminated.

However, on one of the interviews, I spoke with a preacher on a radio station in the Deep South. In contrast to the critics, he really liked *The Shack* and was curious about the negative responses, so I shared with him the cake-poop illustration.

---

102 *Finding God in the Shack* (Biblica, 2009).

He responded without missing a beat: "Professor, I don't see it like that. The way I see it is, reading a book isn't like eating a piece of cake. Rather, it's like eating a piece of fried chicken: you eat the meat and leave the bone!" How right he is. The progressive Christians remind us that all human knowing is *human* knowing and, as such, it is limited in perspective and fallible in outcome.

As the saying goes, to err is human. Set against that backdrop, the heart of the progressive conversation is an embodiment of just what it is to be Christian: seek truth and leave behind the error. Or, if you prefer, eat the chicken, and leave the bone.

5

Doubt

is Not Separate from Disbelief

As I said, I grew up in a conservative evangelical and dis-pensational context very similar to that of Alisa Childers. One of the hallmarks of that upbringing was that we were raised with a strong emphasis on the importance of being certain in our beliefs. For example, the stock Pentecostal greeting I grew up with was "Do you have the *victory* today?!" The answer was supposed to be an unequivocal *"Yes!"* And just to be clear, to have the victory was not to have a doubt. (Can I have an amen?!) This also carried through to street evangelism where we always opened with this line: "Do you know where you'd go if you died tonight?" If we asked you that on the street corner and you didn't know that you'd definitely go to heaven, if you weren't *certain*, you could be prepared to get the full gospel presentation courtesy of me and my street evangelism partner. I was taught that the Christian life was about belief, the stronger the better.

As you can expect, with that kind of backdrop there was a real stigma when it came to those who experienced doubt.

The specter of uncertainty called to mind Doubting Peter who sank into the waves and received the following reprimand from the Lord: "You of little faith, why did you doubt?" (Matthew 14:31) And then there was the even more infamous Doubting Thomas who disbelieved in the resurrection of Jesus when everyone else believed (John 20:24-29). Since faith the size of a measly mustard seed could move mountains (Matthew 17:20) the contrast between the feckless doubter who sinks in a puddle and the stalwart of faith who hurls a billion tons of rock at will could not be greater. Given that the options were to sink in the waves or move mountains, it's hardly surprising that we all longed for certainty.

But here's an important thing to recognize about doubts: people don't *choose* to have them. Rather, they *find themselves with them.* Now, that's not to say that we have no control at all over our beliefs (or doubts). We do make choices that can indirectly shape how we think in all sorts of ways. But the point remains that doubts are not directly under our voluntary control. I certainly don't *choose* to doubt. And with that in mind, telling a person to "just believe" is like telling the clinically depressed person to "just cheer up." Things don't work like that.

Not only does it do no good to stigmatize doubt, but we also need to recognize that just as pain provides important feedback for the body,[103] so doubt provides important feedback for the mind. To that end, I like to tell the following story. Picture a bush plane crashing in the northern woods of Canada in the middle of winter. As the pilot and passenger lie in the snow waiting for their rescue, each finds himself in a very different state. The pilot says "All my bones ache. My hands are killing me. My legs feel a lot of pain!" Meanwhile, the passenger smiles serenely: "I don't feel anything at all! I'm just going to go to sleep here in the snow." Which of these

---

103 Paul Brand and Philip Yancey, *The Gift of Pain: Why We Hurt & What We Can Do About It* (Zondervan, 1997).

two individuals is in worse shape? Obviously, it's the guy who doesn't feel anything because his body isn't responding to his environment anymore. In the same way that pains point to a body responding appropriately to its environment, so doubts point to a mind responding to its environment. As Frederick Buechner memorably put it, "Doubts are the ants in the pants of faith. They keep it awake and moving."[104]

Even as I say that I hasten to add that you would be mistaken to assume that people *need* to have doubts. The assumption that a person must have doubts if they are to have mature faith is as much an error as assuming they *cannot* have doubts to have faith. As Exhibit A, my dad had a deep and steady Christian faith without significant doubt throughout most of his life. And yet, his faith was not necessarily the worse for its absence of doubt just as my faith is not the worse for the presence of doubt.

Rather than raise suspicions about whether other people believe (or doubt) enough, those who believe and those who doubt would be better off thinking of their different orientations toward the doctrines of Christian faith in the manner of Paul's metaphor of the body (1 Corinthians 12:12-31), with each orientation serving the overall health of the church. A couple of years ago, I wrote an entire book cataloguing my own doubts titled *Conversations with My Inner Atheist*. In the book, I described the Christian community in the terms of a sailing ship. Just as the ship needs both ballast for stability and sails to catch the wind, so a Christian community is well served by the presence both of people who have deep and settled convictions (the ballast) and those who doubt and question (the sails). The convictions ground and stabilize the community while the doubts and questions drive the community forward.[105]

---

104 Buechner, "Doubt," https://www.frederickbuechner.com/ quote-of-the-day/2016/10/26/doubt

105 See "Secure the Ballast and Raise the Sail: An Introduction," in *Conversations with My Inner Atheist*, 1-6.

In this chapter, we are going to consider Childers' relationship with faith and doubt. As we will see, she makes some effort to break out of the binary mindset as she acknowledges a limited role for doubt in the Christian life. Unfortunately, she can't quite break free of that binary because she then insists that doubt is categorically different from unbelief and that unbelief is always defined by a morally culpable refusal to believe.

A Positive Word on Doubt, a Potshot at Progressives

I once visited a church that advertised the course "Christianity Explored" with the invitation that it is "a safe place to share your doubts and ask hard questions." My first reaction was, "great, it's good to know they have such a place!" But then it occurred to me: why is Room 212 on Tuesday nights the one safe place to share doubts and ask hard questions? Why isn't the church *generally* a safe place to share doubts and ask hard questions? Childers seems to understand that point as she writes: "If more churches would welcome the honest questions of doubters and engage with the intellectual side of their faith, they would become safe places for those who experience doubt." [106] To that, I say yea and amen, so I commend Childers' recognition of the place of doubt in the Christian life, so far as it goes.

Unfortunately, Childers doesn't stop there. Right after that concession to doubt, she immediately takes a potshot at progressives: "If people don't feel understood, they are likely to find sympathy from those in the progressive camp who *thrive on reveling in doubt.* In progressive Christianity, doubt has become *a badge of honor to bask in, rather than an obstacle to overcome.*"[107] With those words, the binary mindset reasserts itself as Childers claims that progressives don't want to believe and that they value doubt as an end in itself.

---

106 Childers, *Another Gospel?* 51-2.

107 Childers, *Another Gospel?* 52, emphasis added.

Is that fair? Do progressives denigrate belief and elevate doubt *as an end in itself?* As always, I need to restate my standard disclaimer: given that "progressive Christian" is a label for a vast and diverse conversation, it would be a fool's errand to claim that there are no self-described progressive Christians who could possibly match that description. Perhaps there are. In the same way, it would be a fool's errand to insist that there are no self-described evangelical Christians who believe Donald Trump is God's chosen vessel to rid the world of an international conspiracy of pedophiles. No doubt, there are such evangelicals as well.[108] It hardly follows that we should taint all evangelicals with the QAnon brush.

The real question is this: do the thought leaders, the people that Childers takes as *representative* of the conversation, really endorse such a view in which belief is disparaged and doubt is praised as an end in itself? While I don't claim to have read every book touching on the topic by every person who could be considered a thought leader in this broad, vaguely defined group, from what I've seen, the answer is a solid *no.* The overriding concern is not to valorize doubt as an end in itself.

To understand better the origin of Childers' mistaken interpretation, we can return for a moment to the last chapter where she falsely accuses Rob Bell of questioning truth when he was, in fact, only chastening our confident ability to *grasp* truth from our fallible perspective. Once Childers has taken that wrong turn of interpretation (thereby ironically illustrating Bell's point!), it is no surprise that she ends up concluding that progressives attack certainty, that they don't care about (objective) truth, and that they valorize doubt. However, if we follow through on Bell's point, we can see things start to make a lot more sense. Doubt is not an end in itself: rather, it is a tool to give our confidence a healthy and much needed shake

---

108 Kaleigh Rogers, "Why QAnon Has Attracted So Many White Evangelicals," *FiveThirtyEight* (March 4, 2021), https://fivethirtyeight.com/features/why-qanon-has-attracted-so-many-white-evangelicals/

and thereby to get us to become more aware of our blind spots and where we may need to update our beliefs.

As a case in point, consider Peter Enns' provocatively titled book *The Sin of Certainty* which is part of a growing list of books offering a favorable take on doubt.[109] Granted, a quick gander at the title alone might seem to support Childers' claim that progressives view doubt as an "honor to bask in." But let me give you a tip from an author to a reader: as a general rule, book titles are meant to grab your attention while the subtitle should give you a fuller sense of what the book is *actually* about. In terms of grabbing the attention of the potential reader, I'd say "The 'Sin' of Certainty" does very well: it definitely got *my* attention!

But remember, if you want the fuller story, you need to turn to the subtitle, which in this case is *Why God desires our trust more than our 'correct' beliefs.* And right there we can see that the real point isn't that certainty is literally a sin in and of itself. Rather, the point is that instilling too much confidence in a fallible and perspectival theological construction may leave you unwilling to update when new evidence arises that doesn't fit with your paradigm. Thus, we always need to be willing to update our beliefs when they are at loggerheads with reality. Remember that Enns doesn't say God desires our *doubt*. Rather, he says God desires our *trust*. And there may be no time where trust is required more than when you are being challenged to reconsider long held beliefs in the light of new evidence.[110]

---

109 For similar titles, see David Felten and Jeff Procter-Murphy, *Living the Questions: The Wisdom of Progressive Christianity* (HarperOne, 2012); Brian McLaren, *Faith After Doubt: Why Your Beliefs Stopped Working and What to Do About It* (St. Martin's, 2021); A.J. Swoboda, *After Doubt: How to Question Your Faith without Losing It* (Brazos, 2021); Rachel Held Evans, *Searching for Sunday: Loving, Leaving, and Finding the Church* (Thomas Nelson, 2015).

110 For further discussion see the section "What So Sinful about Certainty?" in *The Sin of Certainty: Why God desires our trust more than our 'correct' beliefs* (HarperOne, 2017), 16-19.

Before people spoke of progressive Christians, emergent Christians, or even Brian McLaren's *New Kind of Christian*,[111] there was Dave Tomlinson's book *The Post-Evangelical*. Originally published in 1997, Tomlinson was writing in a British context where he offered a critique of historic Christian fundamentalism and evangelicalism that would anticipate themes developed at length over the next two decades in the American context. His parable of the Evangelical and the Liberal Bishop is a great example with respect to the current topic:

> Jesus told a parable to a gathering of evangelical leaders. "An evangelical speaker and a liberal bishop each sat down to read the Bible. The evangelical speaker thanked God for the precious gift of the Holy Scriptures and pledged himself once again to proclaim them faithfully. 'Thank you God,' he prayed, 'that I am not like this poor bishop who doesn't believe your Word and seems unable to make his mind up whether or not Christ rose from the dead.' The bishop looked puzzled as he flicked through the pages of the Bible and said, 'Virgin birth, water into wine, physical resurrection. These things are hard to believe in, Lord. In fact, I'm not even sure I'm in touch with you in a personal way. But I'm going to keep on searching.' I tell you" said Jesus, "that this other man, went home justified before God. For those who think they have arrived have barely started out, but those who continue searching are closer to the destination than they realize."[112]

Tomlinson intends this passage as a reworking of the parable of the Pharisee and the Tax Collector with evangelicals as the intended audience. Who would've thought that one could have pride in their right doctrine? And yet, the Pharisees

---

111 McLaren, *A New Kind of Christian: A Tale of Two Friends on a Spiritual Journey* (Wiley, 2001).

112 Dave Tomlinson, *The Post-Evangelical*, rev. North American ed. (emergentYS books; Zondervan, 2003), 69-70.

of Jesus' time would never have imagined their meticulous law-fulfillment could've been part of the problem. The truth is that human beings can turn just about anything into an idol. And lest you think the liberals get an easy pass, Tomlinson adds, "the parable cuts both ways: my retelling of the parable for a gathering of liberal churchgoers would be the other way around!"[113]

The Sin of Unbelief . . . But Not Doubt?

Childers may not believe doubt is necessarily sinful, but she does say that unbelief is. Is she correct? The place to begin is with Romans 1:18-20 in which Paul says that God's knowledge is plain to all because his power and nature are knowable through creation so that all people are "without excuse." Based on this passage, Childers concludes that "every person who ever lived not only has knowledge of God's existence but also of his nature and some of his attributes."[114] From this she concludes that "Unbelief is a conscious choice to live as if God does not exist—and it's born out of sinful desires."[115] Thus, Childers wants to argue that while doubt is not sinful . . . or at least not *always* sinful, that is very different from unbelief which is indeed always sinful.

So how does Childers distinguish sinful *unbelief* from non-sinful *doubt*? To be honest, I don't find her explanation to be very helpful. She says: "Unbelief is a decision of the will, but doubt tends to bubble up within the context of faith."[116] I take it that by saying "bubble up" Childers means to say that doubts are *involuntary* whereas unbelief is somehow a matter of the will. She seems to think that Christians can have some

---

113 Tomlinson, *The Post-Evangelical*, 70.

114 Childers, *Another Gospel?* 49.

115 Childers, *Another Gospel?* 49.

116 Childers, *Another Gospel?* 49.

involuntary (and so non-culpable) doubts but as soon as one is not a Christian, one is not engaged simply in doubt within the context of faith, but rather in unbelief. And all *unbelief* exhibits sinful rebellion, an exercise of the will.

Interestingly, Childers doesn't seem to extend this concession for non-culpable doubt to the progressive pastor. She recalls: "One day in class the pastor admitted that in any given moment, he was only 60 to 80 percent certain about Christianity. At first I didn't believe him. *How can a committed Christian, let alone a pastor, be only 60 percent sure? Is this what a 'hopeful agnostic' looks like?*"[117] To be honest, I don't get this response: it's like Childers takes away with the left hand what she just granted with the right. After just recognizing that doubts can be present non-culpably in a Christian's life, she expresses incredulity that doubts can be present in a Christian *pastor's* life. Who says that becoming a pastor suddenly exempts you from serious doubts?

Given that Childers is indignant that a Christian, "let alone a pastor," might be "only 60 percent sure," it raises the question: what percentage of doubt *would* satisfy her as being permissible for a pastor? 30 percent? 20 percent? A mere 10 percent? Unfortunately, she doesn't tell us. However, on the next page she does say that faith is "not a blind leap in the dark, and it's not 100 percent certainty. It is trust based on evidence."[118] I suspect many progressive Christians would agree. But the question remains: for Childers, how much can you fall short of the 100 percent certainty benchmark before being subject to her moral condemnation? And what is so wrong with the pastor who, despite honestly struggling many days at a middling 60 percent conviction, nonetheless trusts God enough each week to climb those steps to the pulpit and proclaim the Gospel once again? Speaking for myself, I am at least as inspired by the pastor who persists despite doubts as

117 Childers, *Another Gospel?* 50.

118 Childers, *Another Gospel?* 51.

the one who never has them. In fact, this sounds a lot to me like what Eugene Peterson used to call *A Long Obedience in the Same Direction.*

The Belief/Unbelief Continuum

We now need to turn our gaze squarely on Childers' attempt to render unbelief as a morally culpable state. It seems to me that her attempt to distinguish unbelief from doubt at this point is simply not defensible or even coherent. In keeping with the binary mindset, Childers approaches the issue as an either/or as if belief is like a light switch: it's either on or off, culpable or non-culpable. Thus, we get two separate categories with doubt qualifying degrees of belief but remaining wholly distinct from unbelief. On this account, one can experience ever accruing doubts bubbling up without culpability, but the second one reaches a threshold of disbelief they are suddenly sinning. But that just doesn't work. If the doubts are involuntary and thus beyond direct culpability, then the *result* of those doubts, that is unbelief, should be as well.

What we have here is a continuum between certainty in the truth of a proposition and certainty in the falsity of that proposition. All degrees of belief and unbelief/doubt exist on that continuum. So, for example, let's say the proposition in question is "Jesus is Lord." Some people are certain that proposition is true, others are certain it is false. Between those two poles is where most people find themselves with respect to most propositions, i.e. as affirming or not affirming, believing or disbelieving the truth of the proposition with various degrees of confidence or conviction. The steps between certainty of belief and certainty of unbelief along this continuum are represented by degrees of belief and/or doubt.

Let's consider some of the factors that are relevant to the complexity of belief:

- *Agnosticism.* The progressive pastor described himself as a hopeful agnostic, much to Childers' chagrin. But for many of us in life, we find that for many things we don't have settled convictions and so we are agnostic, not because we *choose* to be but because the evidence available to us simply does not compel us to a settled conclusion.

- *Fluctuating degrees of assent.* States of belief, unbelief, and doubt are not static. For many of us, we may find ourselves in the space of agnostic doubt some days and with assent rising and falling in cycles in accord with life's circumstances. Many Christians experience spiritual highs in which God seems as plain to them as the nose on their face followed by spiritual lows in which they feel alone and abandoned. (Remember Elijah or John the Baptist?) Belief is not typically static, but rather waxes and wanes such that our current beliefs and doubts are often but a snapshot in time.

- *How what you do maps onto professed belief (and doubt).* One of my colleagues has the following tagline on his emails: you show what you believe by what you do. In other words, *what you say you believe* matters, but *how you act* gives sense to the words you say. Along those lines, think of Jesus' Parable of the Two Sons (Matthew 21).

- *Desire to believe.* Many people may find themselves with beliefs that they *want* to be false. Others may not believe but they *desperately want to.* How does this dimension of desire feature into the equation?

Do you believe Jesus is Lord and that God raised him from the dead (Romans 10:9)? And how strongly do you believe it? 100 percent? 60 percent? Somewhere in between? And remember, such a question is but a snapshot in time, for one can also ask how strongly you believed yesterday . . . or how strong your belief might be tomorrow. Some days it may seem to you that "Jesus is Lord" is as self-evident as the nose on your face. Other days, you may find yourself racked with doubts like the father of Mark 9:24 who cries out, "Lord, I believe. Help my unbelief!" Through it all, do you continue to exercise that long obedience in the same direction *despite* your doubts? And what do you want to be true? Do you *long* for the great things of the Gospel to be true even when you doubt?

Like I said, these matters are complicated and if you want to start factoring in degrees of responsibility you better have a sufficiently complex grid to capture all the dimensions of belief. One thing is clear: it is very important to return to the foundation of Christian belief always remembering that it is not anchored in doctrine (as Strobel and Childers think) but rather in *Jesus Christ*. The issue is less about the set of beliefs you affirm *about Jesus Christ* on a given day or *how strongly you affirm them* than *whether you are continuing to build a relationship with him in the midst of fluctuating belief.* And keep in mind that building a relationship with Jesus is expressed through actions like taking up your cross daily and loving your neighbor as yourself.

Childers' Ambiguity and Atheist Doubt

As we saw, Childers claims that "unbelievers" are immoral because "every person who ever lived not only has knowledge of God's existence but also of his nature and some of his attributes." Thus, she concludes that "Unbelief is a conscious choice to live as if God does not exist—and it's born out of sinful desires."[119] Unfortunately, there is a deep ambiguity in Childers' conception of "unbeliever" and specifically whether it references *those who do not believe in God* (i.e. atheists) or *those who do not believe in Christianity*.

Let's begin with the second option. On this take, the contrast between rebellious unbelief and doubt that bubbles up "in the midst of faith" would suggest that (non-culpable) doubt is that which is experienced by a Christian whereas rebellious

---

119 Childers, *Another Gospel?* 49.

unbelief is that which is experienced by a non-Christian: thus, every single person who is not a Christian is thereby wickedly refusing to become one. And remember, according to Childers this would apply to "every [non-Christian] who ever lived." On this scenario, every person who ever lived is in sinful rebellion against God in all the moments when they are not a professing Christian. This extraordinary judgment would extend to the lovely Jewish rabbi down the street who regularly hosts dialogues with Christians, the third century Chinese Buddhist monk who spent his life serving the poor, the Muslim doctor who wrote the book *I Shall Not Hate* after Israelis killed his family,[120] and the Jewish girl killed by Nazis in Auschwitz. On that account, all these people are rebelliously refusing to become Christians. That seems to me like an incredibly implausible claim.

Now let's turn to the first option. On this take, Childers' contrast with doubt "in the midst of faith" would be directed more narrowly toward those who do not believe that God exists or that he has specific divine attributes. On this account, it is only those folk who would be ripe for moral censure. This take seems to fit far better with the context of Romans 1 in which Paul is not referencing the particulars of Christian doctrine at all but rather a general belief in God's existence and nature. On the downside, this interpretation undermines Childers' attempt to maintain a tidy distinction between doubt and unbelief. If the only areas of disbelief that are subject to moral censure involve the existence of God and some of his attributes, then we cannot automatically stigmatize doubt in all manner of specifically Christian doctrines, from the Trinity to the incarnation to the atonement. Thus, if we take this narrower interpretation, then Childers loses her basis to condemn most of the "unbelief" that arises in the midst of the progressive conversation.

---

120 *I Shall Not Hate: A Gaza Doctor's Journey on the Road to Peace and Human Dignity* (Bloomsbury, 2012).

Not only does the first interpretation undermine the attempt to stigmatize progressive Christian questioning and doubt, but it also entails a moral condemnation of all disbelief in God's existence or attributes. This is highly implausible. We can see this point by considering first how this view would apply to atheists and then how it also has some very problematic implications for Christians.

Let's begin with the application to atheists. On this second reading of Romans 1, all atheists are in sinful rebellion against God because they have knowledge of God that they sinfully suppress. Thus, by saying they don't believe in God they are, in fact, engaged in the bad faith action of denying the existence of the God they *really do believe in*. It is important that we are clear on just what is being proposed here so consider the following analogy. When Jones comes in to work at Denny's, Smith tells her "Tom Cruise came in yesterday for lunch!" Jones is understandably skeptical, so Smith bets her $10 that it's true. "I'll take that bet!" Jones replies. "There's no way a movie star came to our restaurant!" So Smith shows Jones the security camera footage from the previous day that clearly depicts Cruise entering the restaurant with an entourage. Next, she produces a selfie with Cruise that she took on her phone. Finally, she points to an article about the visit on the celebrity gossip website TMZ.

That's excellent evidence for an otherwise very implausible claim, so you would expect Jones to admit defeat and fork over $10 in short order. Alas, Jones is unmoved: "I'm not paying," she says. "That's not Cruise. It's just a lookalike!" In a case like that, Smith could conclude that Jones knows she was wrong, but she refuses to admit it because she is stubborn. On Childers' account, the atheist is like Jones: he *knows* that God exists, but he refuses to admit it because he is sinful.

What should we think of that claim? I have talked to a lot of atheists over the years. And as with many things, the reasons for belief and unbelief in this matter are complicated and very much person-particular. But for our purposes, I simply want to argue a very modest thesis: *not all instances of atheism can be plausibly explained in terms of a sinful rebellion that suppresses an innate belief that God does exist.* In my experience, this simply does not describe the psychological experience and personal narratives of many of the people I have gotten to know over the years. I argue this case at length in my book *Is the Atheist My Neighbor?*[121] But I'm not going to get into my biblical, theological, philosophical, and pastoral arguments here. What I will do is simply invite you to consider some of the complexities of the personal narratives of two people.

Here is the first example. A few years ago, I got to know one of the preeminent atheist philosophers of religion in the world: John L. Schellenberg. Schellenberg is well known in academic philosophy for the development of what he calls the argument from divine hiddenness for atheism. It's a serious argument based on careful logical reasoning and personal experience.[122] A couple of years ago, I interviewed Schellenberg on my blog. In that interview, he described his journey to atheism as follows:

> I was not always an atheist. Indeed, I was a committed evangelical Christian until the age of 22. However university courses in philosophy and religious studies changed my mind. I started university somewhat late, having spent three years at a Bible institute in Alberta (Peace River Bible Institute) and then a year as associate pastor at Foothills Mennonite Church in Calgary. Music was a big part of my life back then, too, and I expected to be involved in Christian ministry, in a variety of different ways. What I was exposed to at university—for the first time—came as a shock, and though I resisted strongly

---

121 *Is the Atheist My Neighbor? Rethinking Christian Attitudes Toward Atheism* (Cascade, 2015).

122 For an introduction to the argument see John L. Schellenberg, *The Hiddenness Argument: Philosophy's New Challenge to Belief in God* (Oxford University Press, 2015).

for a year or so, *doubts and then later disbelief* replaced my Christian belief.[123]

When I hear a story like this, I always seek to exercise the hospitality of carefully listening and accepting the truth of what people say unless I have some overriding reason to believe they are deeply confused or lying. And having heard Schellenberg's story and considered his meticulously formed arguments, I don't see any reason to think he is either confused or dishonest. I certainly don't see evidence that he hates God and is sinfully suppressing his belief in God to justify living contrary to God's law. Rather, I see a brilliant, thoughtful individual who gave more careful consideration to the grounds for belief than most Christians do, and in his case, it led to him losing faith.

To be sure, equally intelligent people have travelled a similar route and ended up with the opposite conclusion. But it is precisely in this moment that we need to resist the temptation of the binary mindset that wants to force us into imputing malevolent motives to those who process their evidence and experience differently than we do. Instead, we need to recognize that people of good will can sometimes end up coming to opposite conclusions even when they assess the same evidence. And I assure you that the existence of God is *not* the only topic where this is true!

Now for the second example: without a doubt, one of the most haunting documentaries I have ever watched is the 2006 Academy Award nominated film *Deliver Us From Evil*. This documentary chronicles the horrifying crimes of Father Oliver O'Grady, a Catholic priest who molested and raped dozens of children in the state of California. After I saw the film, I was haunted by the evils of this man, but the case of one anguished father in particular stayed with me. As a result, I have repeatedly mentioned Bob Jyono in my books.[124] I've never been able to shake his story from my consciousness.

Here's why. Jyono was a pious Catholic who had raised his family in the faith. Then he learned one day that the beloved priest who had served his family for years had repeatedly raped his daughter and that he had done so *in the family home.* After that horrific discovery, Jyono could no longer believe in God. He could not reconcile the idea of a God of perfect love and care with the reality that this same God stood by and did nothing while his daughter was being raped in his house. You can blame Jyono's disbelief upon sinful rebellion if you like. But personally, I think you need more categories to process something like that. I cannot imagine the hell it would be to discover that your beloved child had been repeatedly sexually assaulted by a religious leader in whom you'd placed such great and unqualified trust. Nor can I imagine what it would be like to envision God standing by while that happened. Had that been me, I shudder to think what that might do to my faith.

Tragically, the horror story of Bob Jyono is but one example of countless victims of abuse that have been linked to the Catholic Church. In 2018 the state of Pennsylvania published the results of a massive investigation into clergy abuse. The Pennsylvania Grand Jury Report is an 800-page record chronicling the systemic rape and molestation of children on an industrial scale by hundreds of Catholic priests over decades. The horrors include clergy beating and raping children, making child pornography, hitting children with whips, forcing children to commit sexual acts on priests, and on and on. Many families were victimized multiple times: in one family alone, a priest raped *five girls.* The report begins with this chilling flyover description of the litany of abominations to be described in its pages:

---

124 See *Is the Atheist My Neighbor?*, 84. *You're not as Crazy as I Think,* 200. *Finding God in the Shack,* 116.

Over one thousand child victims were identifiable, from the church's own records. We believe that the real number—of children whose records were lost, or who were afraid ever to come forward—is in the thousands.

Most of the victims were boys; but there were girls too. Some were teens; many were prepubescent. Some were manipulated with alcohol or pornography. Some were made to masturbate their assailants, or were groped by them. Some were raped orally, some vaginally, some anally. But all of them were brushed aside, in every part of the state, by church leaders who preferred to protect the abusers and their institution above all. [125]

In all the horror of that agonizing report, the words of one woman haunt me above all: "The word 'God' makes me think of *him*," she said. Can you imagine what that is like, being in a situation where your thinking about God is hopelessly and inextricably interwoven with the image of the man who raped you as a child?

To loop this awful conversation back into the topic of unbelief and sin, my simple word to all of us is this: it is not right to assume *a priori* that every instance of a person who disbelieves in God's existence or nature is thereby in sinful rebellion against God. Until you've walked in the shoes of other people, it's not your place to speculate on that matter.

Interestingly, Childers' failure to maintain a sharp distinction between unbelief and doubt also surfaces here. Let's consider for a moment that we were to bite the bullet and insist that every John L. Schellenberg who stopped believing after a careful reasoning process and every Bob Jyono who stopped believing after a life crisis is really in sinful rebellion against God. In other words, we're going to stick with Childers' take

---

125 Pennsylvania Diocese Victims Report, https://www.attorneygeneral.gov/report/

on Romans 1 despite the enormous implausibility with this interpretation.

Once we do that, we are in a place to consider the second issue, namely how this view affects *Christians*. The problem is that this interpretation ends up *condemning every instance of doubt that "bubbles up" in the midst of Christian belief* as well. To see why, consider that Paul says in Romans 1:20 (the verse Childers cites to condemn atheists) that God's existence and nature are *kathorao*, a verb meaning to see or perceive clearly or fully. Thus, it is commonly translated as "clearly seen" (KJV, NASB, NIV, CEB, ASV, HCSB, GNT) or "clearly perceived" (ESV; RSV). Here is the problem: if something is clearly seen, then it isn't just the people who *deny it* (i.e. the atheists) who are in rebellion, but also those who profess *not to see it clearly*.

Think again of the bet between Smith and Jones. What if, instead of outright denying that she is wrong, Jones replied by saying "Interesting stuff, but that evidence isn't good enough. I'm not saying it *isn't* Cruise, but I just can't tell from the video, the selfie, and that TMZ story. Sorry, I'm not convinced." In this case, Jones didn't outright deny the evidence, but she does insist, very implausibly, that the evidence isn't sufficient to convince her. In this case, you would still conclude that Jones is being dishonest and reasoning in bad faith. After all, there is more than enough evidence to convince any honest person that Cruise visited the Denny's, so any refusal to accept the evidence. whether that of the outright denial or the doubter, is equally disingenuous. By the same token, if God's existence and nature really are *kathorao* to everyone without distinction, that applies as surely to the Christian in the moment they experience any question or doubt about God's existence or nature as to the atheist who outright disbelieves.

With that in mind, let's shift our attention from Bob Jyono to parents who remained Christians after the discovery that their children had been abused by a predatory priest. While they may have remained Christians, do you think they might have experienced some moments of questioning and doubt in the wake of that living nightmare? It seems to me that that would be a very reasonable response to such a horrifying discovery. And yet, if God's existence and nature really are always *kathorao* then by this logic, those moments of questioning or lingering doubts would be equivalent to Jones refusing to find the evidence adequate to conclude that Cruise visited the restaurant. In short, this position ends up condemning the momentary doubts of a grieving Christian parent as sinful rebellion alongside the atheist. But this can't be right. Not every doubt is automatically sinful. And if that is the case, you can't say that doubts which culminate in unbelief are necessarily sinful either.

Interestingly, Childers seems to want to acknowledge that the issues are far more complex than her analysis would have us think. Thus, for example, she refers to "people who lost their faith because of abuse, doubt, or suffering."[126] Nonetheless, all she can really give us is the unsatisfactory binary analysis that these folk were initially doubting non-culpably (an analysis that we've already seen doesn't work) and then at some point that non-culpable state flipped into morally culpable disbelief. But again, belief/unbelief is not a light switch. The world is just so much more complicated than that, a fact that becomes ever clearer the more you speak to other people and hear their stories for why they do (or don't) believe.

---

126 Childers, *Another Gospel?* 65.

6

Progressive Christians
are Not Gnostics or Marcionites

In this book, we have seen a stark contrast between Childers' view that orthodox Christianity is founded on (or anchored in) doctrine and what I believe to be the correct view that orthodox Christianity is, in fact, founded on and anchored in Jesus Christ. The error is not an insignificant one and it can manifest in all sorts of ways. One of those ways is found in Childers' view that as God progressively reveals himself over time, that revelation must always be given without errors. This assumption is an understandable outcome of Childers' view for if *doctrine* is the foundation of Christian belief and you want a *stable* foundation through time, you can't have it changing in significant respects through the addition *and* subtraction of beliefs. Instead, you need to ensure that there is a constant core of stable doctrine through time.

Progressive Christians see things differently (again, my standard proviso that this is not necessarily a *universally held* perspective, but it certainly is a *representative* one). With the foundation of doctrine being located in a *person*, one is freed up to recognize that the doctrinal understanding of that person and our relationship to them can change over time all while the relationship remains intact. And through those changes we can both acquire new beliefs and come to reject other beliefs as being in error.

Childers attacks progressive Christians for acknowledging the degree to which error can constitute part of our theological understanding over time. She professes to disavow heresy hunting and states that it is the practice of a dour group she describes as hyper-fundamentalists. In fact, Childers herself is a heresy hunter *par excellence* as evidenced in her decision to label progressive Christians with two of the most incendiary heresies of the early Church: Gnosticism and Marcionism. In this chapter we will consider Childers' basis for leveling these extremely serious allegations. Underlying the charges is her refusal to recognize any error in past understanding of doctrine. However, we will see that this is a deeply flawed conception of the progressive nature of revelation and of these specific heresies. In point of fact, that which Childers believes is evidence of heresy is simply the means by which divine revelation accommodates to limited human understanding over time in a manner consistent with perspectivism and fallibilism.

Before we consider Childers' serious allegations of Gnosticism and Marcionism, we should get a working understanding of these two infamous heresies of the early church.

Gnosticism

Gnosticism is an early Christian heresy, but it is also more than that. While it could be enormously diverse in expression, the heart of Gnosticism is found in two central claims: the valuation of spirit over matter and the profession of a secret gospel message given to a select few. Paul Johnson provides a helpful summary description, and note especially how Gnosticism was not a distinct system of thought but rather a parasitic set of

general ideas that could readily glom onto all sorts of religious
systems including Christianity:

> Gnostics had two central preoccupations: belief in a dual
> world of good and evil and belief in the existence of a secret
> code of truth, transmitted by word of mouth or by arcane
> writings. Gnosticism is a "knowledge" religion—that is what
> the word means—which claims to have an inner explanation
> of life. Thus it was, and indeed still is, a spiritual parasite
> which used other religions as a "carrier". Christianity fitted
> into this role very well. It had a mysterious founder, Jesus,
> who had conveniently disappeared, leaving behind a collection
> of sayings and followers to transmit them ; and of course in
> addition to the public sayings there were "secret" ones, handed
> on from generation to generation by members of the sect.[127]

The Christian Gnostics developed their own spiritual writings,
one of the most well-known being the so-called Gospel of
Thomas. This gospel writing is a collection of sayings likely
from the late second century. Saying 13 memorably captures the
gnostic theme that the true Gospel is not a public profession
of Jesus crucified and raised for our sins but rather a secret
knowledge given to a select few:

> (13) Jesus said to his disciples: Compare me, tell me whom
> I am like. Simon Peter said to him: You are like a righteous
> angel. Matthew said to him: You are like a wise philosopher.
> Thomas said to him: Master, my mouth is wholly incapable
> of saying whom you are like.
>
> Jesus said: I am not your master, for you have drunk, and
> have become drunk from the bubbling spring which I have
> caused to gush forth. And he took him, withdrew, (and) spoke
> to him three words.
>
> Now when Thomas came (back) to his companions, they

---

127 Paul Johnson, *A History of Christianity* (Touchstone, 1976), 45.

asked him: What did Jesus say to you? Thomas said to them: If I tell you one of the words which he said to me, you will take up stones (and) throw them at me; and a fire will come out of the stones (and) burn you up.[128]

For a while, the Gnostics battled with the emerging orthodoxy for supremacy, but they were eventually defeated. Irenaeus led the charge against Gnosticism with his book *Against Heresies,* a powerful late second century work that championed the goodness of the material world and insisted that there could be no secret message of salvation since the public Gospel had been given to the Apostles and all those who came after them. With robust arguments like those of Irenaeus, Gnosticism was eventually defeated in the early church.

That said, Gnosticism has continued down through the centuries as a marginal force, always threatening to distort the Christian message with those two parasitic ideas. For ease of reference, we can summarize Gnosticism with respect to these two hallmarks as follows:

- G1: Material creation is bad or less valuable than spirit
- G2: The Gospel message is a secret knowledge given to a select few

Note that Gnosticism, as such, is a very general and broad set of ideas. Though its robust mythological expression was defeated in the early church, it pops up throughout Christian history in these bare ideas, often as a shady influence in otherwise orthodoxy theology. For example, consider this passage from John Calvin: "that man consists of a soul and a body ought to be beyond controversy. Now I understand by the term 'soul' an immortal yet created essence, which is his nobler part."[129]

---

128 "Gospel of Thomas," trans. Blatz, http://www.earlychristianwritings.com/thomas/gospelthomas13.html

129 Calvin, *Institutes of the Christian Religion*, trans. Ford Lewis Battles, ed.

This contrast between the "lesser" corruptible body and the "nobler" immortal soul is suggestive of gnostic influence. Even more striking, Calvin then goes on to describe death as "the soul . . . freed from the prison house of the body."[130] This language of the body as a *prison house* for the soul rather than the natural mode of embodied human existence likewise looks very gnostic.

The impact of Gnosticism on the Christian tradition extends much further than John Calvin. In fact, Christian eschatology has regularly been referred to in terms of "four last things": death, judgment, heaven, and hell.[131] Notably absent from this shortlist is the central Christian eschatological hope of the *resurrection*. As Oscar Cullmann noted in his classic work *Immortality of the Soul or Resurrection of the Dead?*,[132] this historic de-emphasis of the resurrection to a second-tier doctrine in Christian eschatology reflects the long shadow of Platonic (and Gnostic) thought.

The binary mindset thinks that a bit of Gnosticism is like a dollop of poop in the proverbial cake batter: if even a tiny bit of it is mixed in you need to toss the whole cake. By that logic, if we find even a bit of Gnosticism in some progressive Christians then so much the worse for progressive Christianity: send the entire conversation to the same composter as the poop cake! The problem is that by that standard, we would need to toss much of mainstream Christian theology given the gnostic influence on doctrines like the primacy of soul over body and the devaluation of the resurrection of the body. But surely the wiser course is not to think of poop cake but rather the ole chicken and bone. Or as Paul famously put it, test all things and hold onto that which is good (1 Thessalonians 5:21).

John T. McNeil, (Westminster John Knox Press, 1960); (I.15.2),184.

130 Calvin, *Institutes of the Christian Religion*, (I.15.2), 184.

131 See, for example, Fr. Wade L.J. Menezes, CPM, *The Four Last Things: A Catechetical Guide to Death, Judgment, Heaven, and Hell* (EWTN, 2017).

132 (Epworth Press, 1964).

Calvin's anthropology and eschatology may have a gnostic taint, but that doesn't warrant tossing his theology altogether. The same would apply to the gnostic influence in Christian eschatology more generally. And the same goes for whatever gnostic influence may be evident in progressive Christianity.

Having said that, I'm not conceding for a moment that the thought leaders in the progressive conversation are significantly influenced by Gnosticism. On the contrary, it seems to me that several of the leaders of this conversation have offered some deep and penetrating critiques of the gnostic tradition and its influence on Christian theology. For example, Brian McLaren quotes Robert Webber with approval: "Christians are not Gnostics. We do not reject the body, the material, the tangible. To do so would be to reject the incarnation."[133] And in *The Secret Message of Jesus*, McLaren specifically warns against what he calls the church's "love affair with Greek philosophy," and specifically Neoplatonism.[134] Further, McLaren's articulation of the new creation is far more rooted in Hebrew theology than many of the platonic-tinged Christian accounts of a disembodied heaven. (We will return to that topic in chapter 9.)

So far as I can see, when Childers claims that progressive Christians are Gnostics, it is not with respect to a devaluation of the material but rather to the secret knowledge of G2. Rather than allege that they value spirit over body, she seems to limit her critique to the claim that they root salvation in a secret message. We will consider that claim shortly, but for now let us recognize that progressive Christians like McLaren have provided salient *critiques* of the gnostic devaluation of the material. Thus, at a first pass they look to be stalwarts *against* gnostic influence.

---

133 Cited in McLaren, *The Church on the Other Side* (Zondervan, 1998), practice 4.

134 McLaren, *The Secret Message of Jesus* (Thomas Nelson, 2006), 212.

Marcionism

While Gnosticism is a very broad and parasitic set of dispositions, Marcionism is a significantly more precise and comprehensive set of religious claims that trace back to an original founder. Marcion originated in Pontus on the Black Sea and later studied under a gnostic teacher named Cerdo, so it is no surprise that one can see some gnostic elements in his thought including a suspicion of the material world and a belief that the material creation was the product of an inept creator deity. Marcion associated this creator deity with the Hebrew Scriptures and rejected that god along with his capricious divine violence and his unfair favoritism of the Jews. Instead, Marcion embraced what he believed to be the altogether different God of the New Testament, a God that he believed to be universally loving, non-violent, impartial, and to offer a way out of the inept, fallen material world. Marcion also has the distinction of compiling the first official New Testament canon to proclaim his gospel made up of ten Pauline epistles and a truncated version of the Gospel of Luke. However, Marcion rejected the birth narrative in Luke in the belief that God would not be birthed into the world: instead, he believed that Christ was a divine spirit who only appeared human.

As we can see, there are several distinctives of Marcionism which make it significantly more complicated than Gnosticism. These include the following:

- M1: Material creation is bad or less valuable than spirit
- M2: The God of the Old Testament is a capricious, inept, and cruel creator of the material world
- M3: The God of the Old Testament manifested his injustice by unfairly electing Israel
- M4: The New Testament God is good, loves all people, and offers salvation out of the material world

- M5: Jesus was a docetic (i.e. divine but not human) spirit messenger of salvation

Thus, if we are to identify a contemporary Christian as a Marcionite, we should look for evidence of the individual affirming one or more of these claims.

Note as well that G1 and M1 are identical, a point that illustrates the gnostic influence in Marcion's theology. Many Gnostics would also affirm M5. With that in mind, M1 and/or M5 alone would be insufficient to constitute evidence for Marcionism over-against Gnosticism. Thus, to warrant the allegation of Marcionism proper we should look especially for evidence that an individual affirms M2, M3 and/or M4.

Childers, Gnosticism, and Progressive Christianity

Now that we have a working knowledge of both heresies, we can consider the basis for Childers' serious charges. Let's begin with Gnosticism. She claims, "There are many striking similarities between old-fashioned Gnosticism and progressive Christianity."[135] *Many* striking similarities? So far as I can see, Childers actually provides only *one* point, the claim that progressive Christianity allegedly "thrives on viewing itself as a more enlightened and mature version of Christianity."[136] For example, she claims that "McLaren believes that Christians today have a more mature view of God than our predecessors who wrote the Bible did."[137] And she concludes from this fact that "The progressive gospel is Jesus + new knowledge."[138]

As I said, Childers doesn't claim that progressive Christians endorse G1, so everything is dependent on G2. To begin with,

---

135 Childers, *Another Gospel?* 108.

136 Childers, *Another Gospel?* 108.

137 Childers, *Another Gospel?* 109.

138 Childers, *Another Gospel?* 110.

Childers' subjective assessment that progressive Christians allegedly view themselves as "more enlightened and mature" is not evidence of anything. Moreover, I find that assessment to be inconsistent with the epistemic humility in the writings of leading progressive Christians. Furthermore, even if progressives did think their view was more enlightened, that wouldn't of itself constitute any kind of evidence for G2.

Childers' charge presents a serious problem at the outset: while G2 requires *secret knowledge given to a few*, Childers replaces that with *new knowledge* as if simply growing in theological understanding suddenly constitutes evidence of Gnosticism. Based on this switcheroo, she concludes that McLaren's view is gnostic simply because he believes that Christians today have a fuller understanding of God in key doctrinal respects than the biblical authors. This is erroneous reasoning. McLaren's position is merely an acknowledgement of progressive revelation, and yes, that means that Christians today *have* progressed in key respects over the writers of the Old and New Testaments. For example, the biblical authors of the Old Testament did not grasp key doctrines like the Trinity and incarnation. In fact, several Old Testament documents reflect a *henotheistic* worldview (that is, the belief that many gods exist but one god is supreme over the others). Monotheism does not clearly emerge until relatively late in the history of Israel.[139]

Some Protestants will concede that historical development while nonetheless insisting that theological understanding stopped increasing with the faith once for all delivered unto the saints (Jude 3). But the truth is that Jesus promised the Holy Spirit would lead God's people into all truth (John 16:13). And that growth in understanding has continued apace since the completion of the New Testament. For example, the Nicene Creed of the fourth century and the Chalcedonian Definition

---

139 See Mark S. Smith, *The Early History of God: Yahweh and the Other Deities in Ancient Israel* (Eerdmans, 2002).

of the fifth century represent far clearer articulations of the understanding of Trinity and incarnation, doctrines that are present only in seminal form in the New Testament documents. These formal creedal statements were articulated as the culmination of *centuries* of intense theological debate and collective reflection. To say that the bishops at Constantinople in 381 had a fuller understanding of the Trinity or that the bishops at Chalcedon in 451 had a fuller understanding of the incarnation is not "gnostic." On the contrary, the recognition that Christian theological understanding can increase over time is simply a *truism*. To put it another way, if *theological advance over the views of biblical authors* constitutes Gnosticism, then *the entire Christian tradition is gnostic!*

Childers' argument also appeals to examples where progressive Christians identify aspects of the Hebrew Scriptures that are, as she quotes Brian McLaren, "unChristlike." But once again, that isn't a controversial assertion, and it certainly doesn't constitute evidence of Gnosticism. For example, Psalm 37:13 describes God laughing at the coming destruction of the wicked. To say the least, this statement seems to be difficult to reconcile with passages like Ezekiel 18:23 and 2 Peter 3:9 to say nothing of the life and ministry of Jesus. God doesn't *delight* in the destruction of the wicked; rather, God desires none to be lost and all to be saved. It seems to me that passages like Psalm 37:13 are included within the canon of Scripture not to model for us how God thinks but rather to express for us *how human beings sometimes feel*. After all, the Psalms are a record of human experience, and some of that experience is ugly and painful. But we can learn as surely from those darker moments where all-too-human hatreds cloud the psalmist's vision as the penetrating moments where God's supernatural love and forgiveness break through.[140] To be sure, you could insist that my take is not a good one and I've failed to grapple

---

140 For further discussion see Rauser, *What's So Confusing About Grace?* chapter 21.

with Psalm 37:13. But even if that is the case, a failure to interpret a difficult text correctly would not of itself constitute
evidence for *Gnosticism*.

Childers also claims that progressive Christians are like
Gnostics in that "Both claim sources of knowledge outside
the Bible that can and should judge Scripture."[141] It's not clear
what Childers means by "judge scripture." If she means judge
whether a passage should be recognized as scripture, well that's
clearly false. I know of no self-described progressive Christian
who is advocating a redrawing of the canon. And even if there
are such people (again, the conversation is a diverse one so
anything is possible) it doesn't follow that such extreme views
are at all representative.

Conversely, Childers could mean to say that these sources
external to scripture are used to judge *how to interpret* Scripture. But this also isn't helpful because it is completely uncon-
troversial to say that extra-biblical sources can inform the
correct interpretation of Scripture. For example, the rise of the
heliocentric model of the universe forced the church to rethink
how they interpret passages like Joshua 10:13 (God made the
sun and moon stand still) and Psalm 93:1 (the world cannot
be moved). Given that all truth is God's truth, if geocentrism is
shown to be false by good scientific evidence, then it is falsified
as a hermeneutic of Scripture and thus interpretations should
be adjusted accordingly. If the recognition that heliocentric
astronomy should impact theology is enough to make one a
Gnostic, then goodness me, we really are all Gnostics!

To conclude, Childers seems rather confused about what
Gnosticism is. It is *not* the mere claim that doctrinal understanding can improve and increase over time. Rather, as I noted
above, it is defined by a denial of the goodness of material
creation (G1) as well as the claim that the core Gospel message,
information crucial to right relationship with God, is presented
not as a public declaration but rather as a *secret* knowledge

---

141 Childers, *Another Gospel?* 109.

given only to a few (G2). The fact is that Childers provides *no evidence whatsoever* that progressive Christians generally, or Brian McLaren in particular, endorse either of those gnostic claims. In fact, as I noted above, McLaren's writing provides an explicit denial of (G1) and thereby he is an ally to critique much of the wider Christian tradition which *has* been influenced by gnostic thinking.

Childers, Marcionism, and Progressive Christianity

Now let's turn to the question of Marcionism and progressive Christianity beginning with Childers' description of the heresy:

> Marcion began gaining followers and influencing the church. He saw the teachings of Jesus as wholly inconsistent with the mean-spirited, jealous, and wrathful God he perceived in the Old Testament. He believed that the God of the Old Testament and the God of the New Testament were two different deities, with the former being an inferior, wicked, and petty being and the latter being loving and all-forgiving. In stark contrast to the circumcision party, Marcion believed that the Old Testament law was violent and contradictory.[142]

I think that's a reasonably good description of historic Marcionism, though it notably fails to mention M3 or M5.

The concerns begin with the fact that Childers charges progressive Christianity with being "warmed-over Marcionism."[143] To clarify, "warmed-over" means "second hand" or "stale." Thus, it would seem Childers is saying progressive Christianity *is indeed* Marcionite but that it is a new version of an old idea. Notably, calling something warmed-over is not saying it is merely *like* that thing in certain respects but rather that it *is that thing*. Just as yesterday's oatmeal reheated

---

142 Childers, *Another Gospel?* 111.

143 Childers, *Another Gospel?* 112.

in the microwave is the same old thing offered for yet another meal, so the claim that progressive Christianity is warmed-over Marcionism is a claim that it is just Marcionism reheated for a new day.

Having said that, it must be noted that Childers includes a bit of a disclaimer. Rather than say progressive Christianity is "warmed-over Marcionism" full-stop, the complete quote is that it *"looks a bit like* warmed-over Marcionism" (emphasis added). But here's the problem with that qualification. All sorts of things "look a bit like" other things. "Looking a bit like" is not, of itself, of any particular significance. As a case in point, my new puppy *looks a bit like* a gopher. It doesn't follow that my new puppy has any genetic relation to gophers.

Childers' inclusion of that qualification calls to mind the dynamic of trying to have one's cake and eat it too. In this case, make a serious allegation (i.e. "warmed-over Marcionism") while tagging on a qualification that exempts one from needing to provide real evidence to sustain the allegation ("Hey, I only said it *'looks a bit like'* Marcionism!"). That strikes me as deeply disingenuous: if you're going to make a serious allegation, you had better stand behind it. You don't throw around explosive, incendiary theological allegations and then think adding the qualification "looks a bit like" exempts you from having to defend them. If you make the claim, *own it.* (Compare: "Hey, I didn't say Ben *is* a thief. I only said he *acts a bit like* a thief!") Marcionism is a toxic heresy and Childers is wantonly indicting fellow Christians with that heresy. This is a very serious allegation and *one that should never be made unless you are willing to stand behind the claim.*

Also take note that while Childers initially includes a qualification with the charge, that qualification does not appear again over the next four pages (110-13). Instead, she quickly settles into the language of describing progressive Christianity in the terms of Marcionism redux. Thus, despite the initial qualification, it is clear that Childers wants us to believe that progressive Christians are indeed just a tired rehash of the old Marcionite heresy—last night's oatmeal reheated in the microwave—and so it is on that basis that we will assess the evidence for her claim.

Childers primarily defends her claim on page 112. Given that we have defined Marcionism in terms of M1-M5 we should look for evidence that progressive Christians widely accept most if not all of these principles. Do they? Childers provides three lines of evidence, but the truth is that *none* of them specifically references any of M1 to M5. Instead, she invokes different themes which I will number 1-3 under the banner "Childers' Marcionism" (CM):

- CM1: They view "the Old Testament God as petty and spiteful"
- CM2: They deny "God's wrath and hell"
- CM3: They have "discomfort with the blood atonement of Jesus . . ."

Apparently, these three points "look at bit like" Marcionism. But again, my new puppy Timbit looks a bit like a gopher. It doesn't follow that I recently adopted a large rodent. This is a bait and switch, and we should not fall for it. Instead, we should simply refuse to accept CM1-CM3 as providing any evidence of Marcionism as such. Either provide evidence for M1-M5 or withdraw the allegation.

My preliminary conclusion is that Childers has *no evidence* that progressive Christianity is Marcionism warmed-over and saying it *looks a bit like* that is borderline meaningless. That said, I do want to take a closer look at the lines of evidence she does present for CM1-CM3. In the next section, I am going to take on CM1 directly. But first, I want to say a word about CM2 and CM3.

Let's begin with CM2. Childers claims that progressive Christians deny "God's wrath and hell." Again, even if that were true, it just wouldn't constitute evidence of Marcionism as such. Furthermore, *it isn't true*. While I will make the point at much greater length in chapter 9, for now I will simply note that leading progressive Christians generally direct their criticism not toward the concept of hell per se, but rather toward the theory of posthumous judgment in terms of *eternal conscious torment,* a view according to which those outside Christ are resurrected to an eternity of torture in hell. In its place, progressives frequently defend one of the two historic alternatives to eternal conscious torment: annihilationism or universalism, both of which are well ensconced within historic orthodoxy dating back to the Patristic age. Again, criticizing or rejecting eternal conscious torment does not of itself constitute evidence of Marcionism.

As for the allegation of CM3 that progressive Christians are uncomfortable with "the blood atonement of Jesus", this too is simply a confused allegation. Progressive Christians do not reject the atonement *per se,* nor do they have "discomfort" with it (whatever that means). Rather, they generally critique and reject the penal substitutionary theory of atonement. And that is something that many Christians have done. Whether you date the penal substitutionary theory to John Calvin in the sixteenth century (as many historical theologians do) or you believe the theory can be found (at least in protean form) in the Patristics, it has always had critics. Criticizing penal substitutionary atonement just is not the same thing as endorsing Marcionism. For further discussion on this point, see chapter 8.

In addition, Marcion himself professed to revere the writings of Paul and to consider him to be the one true apostle of the spirit teacher Jesus. Marcion held to a particular understanding of Christ's atoning work in which Jesus Christ is believed to have purchased human creatures from death. Given that Marcionism includes a doctrine (if not theory) of "blood atonement," it makes little sense to define Marcionism with respect to a *denial* of blood atonement.

Punishment will drive out rebellion,
but use a sebet to do it

In the last section, I refuted Childers' argument with respect to CM2 and CM3. Now I want to turn to CM1, the claim that the "Old Testament God" is "petty and spiteful." This claim is deserving of a bit more attention because it comes closest to the historic meaning of Marcionism with regard to the opposition between the testaments and the divine beings who allegedly stand behind each testament. The starting point of the allegation here is that progressive Christians are challenging how God is depicted in portions of the Hebrew Scriptures and this, in turn, entails an endorsement of Marcionism.

With that in mind, let's take a closer look at a couple of the factors that lead Christians to rethink how to interpret biblical passages beginning with a verse that Childers herself quotes with glowing approval: Proverbs 22:15. "A youngster's heart is filled with rebellion, but punishment will drive it out of him."[144] Childers recalls that she memorized this verse as a child and labelled it one of the "good verses." She might've had a different assessment had she read a more accurate translation. The translation Childers uses renders the proverb as referencing generic *punishment,* but the actual text is more specific: the Hebrew references use of a *sebet,* that is a rod or stick which is used to physically *beat* a person. In other words, *a stick or whip* will drive out rebellion. As the KJV puts it: "Foolishness is bound in the heart of a child; but the *rod of correction* shall drive it far from him." To be sure, the proverb *is* teaching the importance of exercising stern authority *in general,* but it communicates that general point by commending the prudence of a *specific* action: *physically beating children with a sebet.* So,

---

144 Childers, *Another Gospel?* 115.

ask yourself: is physically beating children an effective way to raise them?

William Webb asked himself that question. In his book *Corporal Punishment in the Bible,* he studies the teaching of the biblical authors on corporal punishment with great care and he illustrates powerfully that several biblical authors echo this teaching that it is wise to beat children (slaves too, by the way).[145] Suffice it to say, in our day such actions would get you arrested for child abuse. Webb also helpfully points out the many ways that conservative Christians end up distorting the teaching of the biblical authors in an effort to make the text align more closely with current attitudes toward corporal punishment, the premiere example being the way Focus on the Family has endorsed corporal punishment as open-handed spanking of small children as if that is the equivalent of beating slaves and children with a switch. (Spoiler alert: it isn't.)

Examples like this one understandably lead progressive Christians to recognize that there are indeed incorrect views expressed by biblical authors: while we can agree with the need for *disciplining* children, we do not agree that *beating* them is the way to do it. At this point, we need to acknowledge where there are errors of morality and prudence present in the text rather than to hide those problems behind our chosen Bible translation. Suffice it to say, it would be absurd to accuse a scholar like Webb of being a Marcionite simply because he does not accept the teaching of some biblical authors that parental authority is best exercised by way of physical beatings.

Genocide?

The issue of corporal punishment is a serious matter given that generations of children have been raised on beatings due, at least in part, to a perceived biblical mandate. As troubling

145 William J. Webb, *Corporal Punishment in the Bible: A Redemptive-Movement Hermeneutic for Troubling Texts* (InterVarsity Press, 2011).

as mandates to beat your children may be, other moral content in the Bible is far more disturbing. At this point, we will consider one of those other areas, namely the biblical warfare texts that describe God as commanding and commending the eradication of entire people groups including the Amalekites (1 Samuel 15) and Canaanites (e.g. Deuteronomy 7:2-5; 20:16-18). These shocking texts appear to describe actions that meet the contemporary legal definition of genocide, so how should we think about them? Beating children is bad enough, but slaughtering them?

Many Christians argue that God did not, in fact, command or commend these violent actions and Brian McLaren is one of them. Childers counters that the problem is not as bad as it seems. She claims that "God commanded Israel to 'utterly destroy' the Canaanites under very special circumstances. Israel was God's chosen people, and they had a unique covenant with him that no one else had." Thus, "his command to 'utterly destroy' the Canaanites was a one-time deal."[146]

All good?

Um, no. These are poor, half-baked responses to a serious problem. To begin with, actions like the mass genocidal slaughter of civilians appear to be intrinsically evil. If you don't believe me, read the accounts of genocide in journalist Philip Gourevitch's *We Wish to Inform You That Tomorrow We Will be Killed with Our Families: Stories from Rwanda*.[147] And ask yourself, are those actions, actions in which civilian men, women, children, and the elderly are mercilessly butchered, are they the kind of actions that are only *potentially* immoral like the act of hitting someone? Or are they rather *intrinsically* evil like the action of raping someone? I believe the moral intuitions of properly functioning human beings strongly support the conclusion that the action of genocidal slaughter is to be classed in the latter category: namely, as intrinsically

---

146 Childers, *Another Gospel?* 174.

147 (Farrar, Straus and Giroux, 1999).

evil. And in that case, it makes no more sense to justify the mass genocidal killing of civilians by appeal to "very special circumstances" than it would make sense to justify rape by appeal to "very special circumstances." Some actions are *intrinsically wrong irrespective of the circumstances* and the act of genocide would certainly seem to be one of those actions.

Childers clearly disagrees. She insists that God's command to eradicate the people of Canaan constituted "a specific act of judgment on an evil nation."[148] Christians who defend the Canaanite genocide regularly appeal to this line by claiming that the slaughter was a just judgment on an evil nation. The Canaanites were so wicked, they claim, that the entire population all had to be slaughtered: not just soldiers but also poor farmers and their wives, small children, infants, the elderly, sick and weak, and the severely mentally and physically handicapped. And all those who weren't slaughtered were to be driven out of the land in a mass ethnic cleansing because of the collective evil of their society.

In his essay "We Don't Hate Sin So We Don't Understand What Happened to the Canaanites,"[149] apologist Clay Jones argues this line by insisting that we are averse to the idea of God commanding the mass killing of women, children, and infants because we are *insufficiently holy*. If we were more like Jesus, he believes, we would appreciate the moral rightness in the act of butchering Canaanite women, children, and infants in his name. In a similar vein, Bible scholar Jack Deere defends the genocidal killing of Canaanites by arguing that they were a "moral cancer" such that "even one of them—even a child left alive—had the potential of introducing an idolatry and immorality which would spread rapidly among the Israelites and bring about the destruction of God's own people."[150]

---

148 Childers, *Another Gospel?* 174-5.

149 *Philosophia Christi*, 11 (2009), 53-72.

150 "Deuteronomy," in *Bible Knowledge Commentary: Old Testament,* Roy B. Zuck and John Walvoord, eds. (David Cook, 1983), 276.

I understand what Jones and Deere are saying. But as for Jones, I think it is incredibly implausible to claim that my revulsion to the butchering of civilians is due to the fact that I don't "hate sin" enough. On the contrary, it seems to me that if our moral knowledge is to be found anywhere it is here in the conviction that civilian men, women, children, and infants *shouldn't be* hacked apart in the name of the Lord. And as for Deere's claim that these human beings were like cancer cells, I will point out that describing human beings as a disease or pestilence in order to justify their slaughter is among the oldest rhetorical justifications for crimes against humanity.[151] Indeed, Deere's description of individual children as being equivalent to cancer cells is reminiscent of Adolf Hitler's description of the Jewish people as a "racial tuberculosis." When Christians begin invoking the worst dehumanizing and objectifying rhetoric of genocide, you know something has gone seriously awry.

While I have no sympathy with the views of Childers, Jones, or Deere, I want to underscore that the point of this discussion is not to endorse a specific view of how to interpret biblical violence or to reconcile our moral intuitions (and commitment to the peaceable Christ) to specific violent biblical texts. (For those interested in pursuing that debate at much greater length, see my book on this topic: *Jesus Loves Canaanites*.[152]) Instead, the main point here is to highlight that simply disagreeing with Childers (and Jones and Deere) does not thereby qualify one as a Marcionite. That's it. That's the point.

The truth is that Christians have debated texts of biblical violence since the early church. Notably, in the Patristic era theologians like Origen and Gregory of Nyssa first developed theologically and ethically motivated non-violent readings of

151 See David Livingstone Smith, *Less Than Human: Why we demean, enslave, and exterminate others* (St. Martins Press, 2011).

152 *Jesus Loves Canaanites: Biblical Genocide in the Light of Moral Intuition* (2 Cup Press, 2021).

these troubling texts. And many other Christians have contributed to that conversation ever since.

With that in mind, we need to call out Childers' question to the progressive Christian, "Have we just now, two thousand years later, discovered the right way to read it?"[153] At this point, as in so many others in the book, she conveys the false impression that there has been some unbroken unanimity of opinion on a particular topic down through theological history, in this case, the question of how to interpret biblical violence. The clear intent is to discredit progressive Christian alternative proposals with the suggestion that they are introducing some wholly new way of thinking about the topic. But this is false: as I just pointed out, there is a long history of debate over how to interpret biblical violence back to the Patristic era.

Finally, we need to underscore once again that it is false and profoundly uncharitable to label mere disagreement over how to interpret texts of biblical violence as entailing Marcionism since one can explicitly deny M1-M5 while still believing that one should seek alternative non-violent interpretations of violent biblical texts. When Gregory of Nyssa, one of the fathers of Nicene Orthodoxy, denied the historic killing of the Egyptian firstborn in his *Life of Moses*, his contemporaries didn't denounce him as a Marcionite. No doubt, this is because they knew what Marcionism is and that Gregory did not endorse it. The truth is that calling Christians like McLaren "Marcionites warmed over" because they explore non-violent readings of violent biblical texts is nothing more than name-calling, poisoning the well, and yet more slander.

Progressive Revelation and Accommodation to Error

Thus far, I have sought to rebut Childers' attempt to taint progressive Christians with the toxic brushes of Gnosticism and Marcionism. To conclude the discussion, I want to focus

---

153 Childers, *Another Gospel?* 110.

on one remaining critical issue underlying her critique and
that is her attempt to embrace the concept of God's progressive revelation over time while insisting that this progression
never includes any accommodation to errant understanding.
Childers sets up her position with a description of the ill-fated
class run by the progressive pastor:

> A consistent theme in our class with the progressive pastor
> was that the earliest Christians represented Christianity in its
> infancy. The thinking went something like this: We wouldn't
> expect a brand-new baby to know everything he will know
> when he's full grown, or to have come out of the womb run-
> ning. First, he must learn to crawl and then to walk. So why
> would we expect people of a newborn religion to have the
> same understanding they would have two thousand years
> later?[154]

Childers takes issue with this idea of a developing theological
understanding that moves, as she puts it, from "crawling"
to "walking." She believes the progressive Christian thereby
naively rejects prior understandings of theology due to some
benighted chronological snobbery.

But as we have already seen, it is undeniable that there
has been theological progress and advance over time: from
ancient Israel's beginnings in henotheism to the monotheism
of the later Hebrew Scriptures to the seminal development of
trinitarian and incarnational theology in the New Testament
to the fuller articulation of those theologies at the councils of
Constantinople (381) and Chalcedon (451), to the move from
geocentric to heliocentric models of the universe, Judeo-Christian theology has always been defined in terms of progress,
innovation, and adaptation. And along the way, progress inevitably includes the recognition that older ideas were, to some
degree, *in error*. Consequently, when Jews became monotheists,

---

154 Childers, *Another Gospel?* 137.

they came to recognize earlier henotheistic theology as being *in error*. When they came to accept a general resurrection after death, they thereby rejected the idea of a permanent disembodied shadowy existence in sheol as being *in error*. When Christians accepted heliocentrism, they came to recognize geocentrism as being *in error*. And so on.

Childers acknowledges the process of progressive revelation: "we *do* see God revealing more about himself throughout the history of the world."[155] However, she then takes away with the left hand what she just gave with the right when she adds: "But it doesn't mean that the revelation progressed from error to truth."[156] It is at this point that we come to a critical error in Childers' thinking. In her view, progressive revelation is like "bricks stacked on top of one another forming a wall of a building."[157] On this account, each new brick of understanding that is added to the wall forever remains and provides the foundation for additional bricks. No deconstruction or removal of bricks is ever required in the continued building of the wall.

This is a deeply misguided understanding of theological development. As I just pointed out, if you hold to a henotheistic understanding of the divine, then a move from henotheism to monotheism is not merely the addition of a new brick—"there is one God"—but also *the removal of other bricks* such as "There are many gods" and "Yahweh is not unique" and "Moloch is a god." That just is the history of Judeo-Christian theology. It is the history of adding bricks and *removing others* and if you remove particular bricks, it is because those bricks were *in error*.

Here's another big example: countless Christians think of God as a temporal being who experiences emotions, undergoes emotional changes, changes his mind, and alters his plans in response to human choices. And it is not surprising that they

---

155 Childers, *Another Gospel?* 138.

156 Childers, *Another Gospel?* 138.

157 Childers, *Another Gospel?* 138.

should think this given that many biblical texts describe God in just these terms. So, it would understandably be a shock to many a Christian layperson to learn how many Christian theologians have insisted instead that God is outside time, completely immutable, impassible, and has no real relation to creation. Clearly, *somebody* is in error here.

One area where this is undoubtedly the case is in the interface between theology and science. The example I gave above concerned the seventeenth century shift from a geocentric view of the universe to a heliocentric one. This shift affected all sorts of doctrines including heaven, the intermediate state, ascension, session (that term refers to Christ sitting at the right hand of the Father), and the second coming of Christ. And thus, it required the removal of several doctrinal bricks to be replaced by others.

Another area concerns the space of ethics and moral action. Again, I noted the case above of corporeal punishment. Several biblical authors commend the act of physically beating children (and slaves) in order to ensure prosocial behavior and good character. And yet, today we recognize that this is a profoundly flawed and abusive understanding of discipline and child rearing. I dearly hope you don't have any slaves, but if you do, beating them merely compounds your moral errors.

I also cited the topic of biblical violence in terms of the genocide of people groups like the Amalekites and Canaanites. To this end, Childers quotes Peter Enns: "The Bible is an ancient book and we shouldn't be surprised to see it act like one. So seeing God portrayed as a violent, tribal warrior is not how God is but how he was understood to be by the ancient Israelites communing with God in their time and place."[158] Childers suggests that with statements like this, progressive Christians are thereby abandoning the Scripture as God's inspired word: "progressives believe we can now read the Bible . . . not as the

---

158 Cited in Childers, *Another Gospel?* 158.

authoritative word of God, but as our predecessors' spiritual travel journal."[159]

But this is a simply a false dilemma: there is no inconsistency between recognizing that God sovereignly incorporated the "spiritual travel journals" of his followers of the past into his authoritative word. Childers would know that if she had read Enns' book *Inspiration and Incarnation* in which he carefully provides a framework to recognize both the full humanity and the full divinity of the text. And don't just take my word for it. Consider this endorsement for the second edition of *Inspiration and Incarnation* from the highly respected Reformed biblical scholar Tremper Longman:

> Peter Enns has done the evangelical church an immense service by challenging preconceived notions of what the Bible ought to be by insisting on building his high view of Scripture on what God intended Scripture to be. When the first edition appeared, it started important and healthy conversations about the Bible in spite of efforts to dismiss or marginalize Enns's viewpoint. One does not have to agree with all his conclusions to understand why this book has helped and will continue to help many people to embrace Scripture as God's Word to us.[160]

Childers doesn't need to agree with McLaren or Enns or other progressive Christians in how to resolve issues like the nature of God, the interface of theology and science, or the problem of biblical violence in ethical issues ranging from corporal punishment to genocide. All I would ask is that she recognize at the very least that *they have a place at the table* of conversation. To attempt to marginalize their voices and exclude them from the conversation by calling them Gnostics or "a bit like

---

159 Childers, *Another Gospel?* 155.

160 Longman, Endorsement of *Inspiration and Incarnation*, back cover.

warmed-over Marcionism" is nothing more than an attempt
to poison the well of discourse.

At one point in the book when Childers is critiquing those
so-called hyper-fundamentalists that she lampoons as "heresy
hunters," she observes, "We need to be diligent about spotting
elements from other heresies that reappear at various times
throughout church history."[161] True enough. But having said
that, you also need to be diligent about *understanding the positions of other people* and *recognizing the nature of theological
reflection itself* and *not slandering others and poisoning the
well with spurious charges of heresy*. In this regard, I believe
that Childers has fundamentally failed. And in doing so, she
has fomented unnecessary division and harmed and hampered
crucial conversations with fellow Christians.

---

161 Childers, *Another Gospel?* 112.

7

Biblical Inspiration

Does Not Extend to Interpretations

Perhaps you've heard this quip: "The Bible may be inerrant, but your interpretation is not." That simple but critically important statement captures the theme of this chapter. Alas, time and again, Childers appears to be unable to distinguish between the Bible and *her interpretation of it* (which is definitely not inerrant). For example, she opens the ominously titled section "Trouble with the Bible" with the statement that some people "have trouble with the Bible itself."[162] And the example that Childers gives us is Rachel Held Evans expressing concern about the Canaanites and biblical violence more generally. Childers notes that Evans wrestled with the problem like this: "If God was supposed to be the hero of the story, then why did God behave like a villain?"[163] Childers then concludes this is evidence that Evans has "trouble" with the Bible.

To say the least, this is deeply uncharitable. If there is trouble afoot, it is not with the Bible *per se* but rather with *how to*

162 Childers, *Another Gospel?* 55.

163 Cited in Childers, *Another Gospel?* 56.

interpret and apply it. This is not hard to understand: if the holy text of a non-Christian religion depicted the religion's deity as commanding followers to slaughter civilian populations in their god's name, you can bet that Christians would use that as evidence for the immorality of the religion. By the same token, texts like Deuteronomy 20:16-18 and Joshua 6 present a similar problem for Christianity. Acknowledging that fact is nothing more than *intellectual honesty.*

That said, Childers offers a two-pronged response to Evans which is presumably meant to hammer home that Evans' concerns are not legitimate and thus her trouble really is with the Bible itself. The first part consists of offering an apologetic defense of a particular reading of the troubling passages. Childers follows this up with an attempt to discredit alternative readings. In this chapter we will take a closer look at both lines of argument before drawing some conclusions.

Explaining (away) Biblical Genocide

Childers' first approach is to offer a defense of a particular reading of the passages that trouble Christians like Evans. Keep in mind that Childers' alternative must be so strong that it simply overwhelms all plausible alternatives. You see, if she cannot clear the field of alternatives due to the sheer force of her reading, then she cannot dismiss other readings as being motivated by trouble with the Bible itself rather than merely her interpretation of it. So does she meet that lofty threshold?

Childers begins with a claim that we already encountered in the previous chapter: some communities can be so sinful that the only response to them is to seek to wipe out the entire society, including all the men and women and even small children and infants that make up that society. This is how she puts it: "the Canaanites were so evil—so remarkably vile in their rebellion against God and all that is good—that if they were alive today most of us would be crying out for justice, seeking to put a stop to their actions by whatever means necessary."[164] The problem is that Childers assumes that "whatever means necessary" includes the wholesale slaughter of men, women, children, and infants which is precisely the question at issue. It seems to me that it takes a particularly audacious instance of gaslighting to try to convince people that the most just response to a wicked society is the mass slaughter of an entire population up to and including newborn infants.

However, could it be that my response misses the point? What if the act wasn't genocide in the first place? Childers explores that line of argument (a claim she borrows from apologist Paul Copan[165]) by claiming that "It's likely that Jericho was more of a military outpost consisting of mostly male soldiers than a type of village where women and children lived."[166] Thus, perhaps what Joshua is actually describing is not a genocide at all but rather something closer to conventional soldier-on-soldier warfare.

Copan's point about the cities is partially true: *most* of the civilian population of Canaan would have lived in the countryside while settlements like Jericho and Ai would have been primarily military and governmental centers of power. However, Childers' attempted rebuttal still fails for several reasons. First, regional military and governmental outposts still *include many civilians*, and that is undeniably the case with settlements like Jericho and Ai. Just read the texts! For example, Joshua 6:21 describes the Israelite soldiers as devoting the entire city of Jericho to wholesale slaughter including "men and women, young and old, cattle, sheep and donkeys." Not only does the text mention the killing of women but also the young (Hebrew *na'ar*: boy, child) and old (Hebrew *zaqen*: old man, elders, old people) and even *animals*. Not only does the text describe the Israelites butchering small children and

---

164 Childers, *Another Gospel?* 57.

165 Childers, *Another Gospel?* 57, 259.

166 Childers, *Another Gospel?* 57.

elderly people along with the adult civilians and livestock, but the description "utterly destroyed" is a translation of the Hebrew *haram* which refers to the giving over to destruction in a cultic act of worship. In other words, the destruction of Jericho is described not only as a military invasion but also as a *mass sacrifice of human beings and animals to Yahweh.*[167]

The same pattern is repeated later in Ai. After the Israelites draw the soldiers away from the settlement (Joshua 8:24), they return to the city to kill all the remaining civilians within the walls, "twelve thousand men and women . . . all the people of Ai." (v. 25) Even if you conclude that the numbers are likely exaggerated, the text still unequivocally describes the mass slaughter of a civilian population of men, women, and (we can assume) children. And again, the theological context for this horrific carnage is *haram* killing, in effect, a mass sacrifice offered to Yahweh.

Perhaps you are okay with that. Maybe you still think that Childers offers a satisfactory rebuttal to the concerns of Evans and others. But even in that case, can it really be said that Childers' argument is so absolutely compelling that the only conclusion is that those who disagree with her have trouble with the Bible itself rather than her interpretation of it? All I can say is I don't see her arguments having that strength at all. On the contrary, I find them flimsy and superficial. I don't have a problem with the Bible, though I have a lot of problems with Childers' interpretation of it.

In Search of the Plain Sense

In my book *Jesus Loves Canaanites* I explore various alternative interpretations of the Canaanite genocide texts and other texts of biblical violence. These include ancient allegorizing (e.g. the above-mentioned Origen and Gregory of Nyssa), what I call

---

167 See Susan Niditch, *War in the Hebrew Bible* (Oxford University Press, 1993), 41.

modern spiritualizing (e.g. Douglas Earl and Jerome Creach) and a view I call providential errancy in which God sovereignly incorporates morally and theologically errant perspectives of the divine nature and action into Scripture (e.g. Greg Boyd). The providential errancy position is also implicit when I suggested that Psalm 37:13 presents an errant perspective of God as vindictive and delighting in the destruction of human beings.

Childers does not interact with any of these alternative views; assuming she is aware of the range of alternatives, this dismissive attitude suggests she doesn't view them to be even worthy of consideration. Part of the reason for that, I suspect, is because I don't think she has seriously grappled with the problem itself. When you carefully reflect on what genocide looks like on the ground and thus what it means for soldiers to engage in the mass slaughter of men, women, small children, and infants, that has a way of focusing the mind.

I suspect that Childers views such alternative ways of interpreting the text as simply beyond the realm of plausibility. That attitude seems to be implicit in her appeal to what she calls the "plain sense" of the biblical text. As she puts it, "What does it mean to take the Bible literally? I've heard it said that it means to read the Bible *literately*. I agree. It means *reading the Bible in the plain sense in which it's written*."[168] Ancient allegory, modern spiritualizing, and providential errancy interpretations of the biblical text all arguably depart from the *plain* sense which would require that Deuteronomy and Joshua be read as simple historical accounts of past events. Perhaps in that sense Childers can return to her insistence that progressive Christians like Evans are really against the Bible rather than merely being against Childers' interpretation of it.

While that would appear to be how Childers thinks, the truth is that matters are far more complicated than that type of argument would suggest. In response, I'm going to consider two points: first, the so-called plain sense is much more

---

168 Childers, *Another Gospel?* 61, second emphasis added.

complicated than Childers recognizes; second, to the extent that one can identify a plain sense of the text, it is a *starting point* rather than an *end point* for interpretation and application.

Let's begin with the first point. In chapter 4, I interacted with the bumper sticker maxim that declares: "God said it. I believe it. That settles it." At that point, I noted that the following much longer maxim that I once saw on a T-shirt is, in fact, far more accurate:

God said it.

I interpreted it
As best I could in light of all the filters imposed
by my upbringing and culture,
which I try to control for
but you can never do a perfect job.

That doesn't exactly settle it,
But it does give me enough of a platform
to base my values and decisions on.

The fact is that we are often inclined to read texts in a way that *we* think is the perfectly obvious "plain sense." But, in fact, we may completely miss aspects of the text which would have been grasped by the original reading audience. As a case in point, I grew up reading Genesis 1 and 2 as straightforward accounts of the creation of the world in a literal 6 24-hour days. What I didn't realize was that this was, in fact, a particular historically conditioned way of reading the text and was nowhere near as neutral and "plain" as I had supposed.[169] It turns out that what we often take to be transcultural plain interpretations which will appeal to all people and all times are, in fact, historically

---

169 See, for example, Ronald Numbers, *The Creationists: From Scientific Creationism to Intelligent Design*, expanded ed. (Harvard University Press, 2006).

conditioned and all-too-fallible perspectives. While that fact doesn't justify us in concluding that we can't get at the original meaning, it does require us to embrace a dose of humility that cautions us against assuming too easily that what we think is the right reading really is that plain.

Since we've been talking about Joshua and biblical violence, let's consider an example of so-called plain interpretation from the book of Joshua. In chapter 10:11-13 we read the following:

> As they fled before Israel on the road down from Beth Horon to Azekah, the Lord hurled large hailstones down on them, and more of them died from the hail than were killed by the swords of the Israelites.
>
> On the day the Lord gave the Amorites over to Israel, Joshua said to the Lord in the presence of Israel:
> "Sun, stand still over Gibeon,
> and you, moon, over the Valley of Aijalon."
> So the sun stood still,
> and the moon stopped,
> till the nation avenged itself on its enemies

It would seem at first blush that the "plain reading" is that God first hurled down large hailstones to kill the enemies of the Israelites and then he stopped the sun and extended the day to give the Israelites time to finish the job. Simple, right?

Maybe not. If someone tells you "It was raining cats and dogs" the plain interpretation for the average English speaker is that this is a figure of speech which means it was raining heavily. For that reader, *the metaphorical interpretation is the plain sense* because they are *familiar* with it. However, a person who was unfamiliar with the idiom could very well draw a very wrong interpretation. For example, they might imagine not thunderclouds heavy with rain but rather a painfully literal situation such as an airplane that somehow lost its load of suburban pets, leaving them to fall from the sky all over the landscape.

As Paul Copan and Matthew Flannagan point out, Joshua's descriptions of hailstones raining down on enemies and a day extended to win a battle are *common literary motifs* in Ancient Near Eastern war accounts and as such, for the reader familiar with those idioms, the plain meaning would be that the tribe's chosen deity intervened on their behalf to win the battle. [170] In other words, it seems likely that the original audience would have been no more inclined to interpret these descriptions *literally* than we are inclined to interpret a statement about raining cats and dogs literally. And that illustrates that we need to be careful about presuming that we have reliable access to what qualifies as a plain reading of ancient texts written in alien languages and set against the backdrop of a distant socio-cultural period.

While cultural distance is one significant obstacle in getting at the "plain" meaning, the distance of translation is another. Keep in mind that reading in translation is only as good as the translation you are reading, and no translation is perfect. As a result, you may think a meaning is plain because of a misleading translation. Consider again the example of Proverbs 22:15. As we saw above, Childers cites a translation of the passage that says, "A youngster's heart is filled with rebellion, but punishment will drive it out of him." However, the translation "punishment" conceals the fact that the Hebrew refers to a stick and thus the act of *beating*. In other words, the plain meaning is not limited to an abstract conception of punishment, but to actual corporeal punishment by physical beating. That is the "plain sense" of the text, and yet it is concealed from many English readers because of the translation. We could easily multiply such examples but suffice it to say, "God said it. I believe it. That settles it" just doesn't cut it.

---

170 Copan and Flannagan, *Did God Really Command Genocide? Coming to Terms with the Justice of God* (Baker, 2014), 97.

This brings us to the second point: *the plain sense is a starting point rather than an end point*. In other words, God can intend to do much more with a text than what is available on the surface. Theologians call that fuller meaning the *sensus plenior* or fuller sense of the text. Consider an example drawn from prophecy. Hosea 11:1 declares "Out of Egypt I called my son." The "plain sense" of that passage is a reference to the history of Israel leaving Egypt. However, Matthew 2:15 goes beyond that meaning to identify a fuller meaning in Hosea 11:1 as a messianic prophecy in which Christ is the new Israel who will also leave Egypt.

Now you might be thinking: "Okay, fine, that was a *Holy Spirit inspired* new meaning. We can allow that. But we uninspired interpreters are *not* authorized to pose additional meanings that go beyond the plain sense!" However, that claim is flatly false: Christians do this all the time. Let's return to the topic I mentioned above regarding how God is often described in very human terms in Scripture. For example:

- In Genesis 22:12 God tells Abraham: "Now I know that you fear God, because you have not withheld from me your son, your only son." The plain meaning of that passage would seem to be that God didn't know initially how Abraham would respond and thus he *learned*.

- In 2 Kings 20 God declares that Hezekiah will die. Hezekiah then pleads for more life, and God subsequently relents and says the king will live fifteen more years (v. 6). The plain meaning of the passage clearly suggests that God *changed his mind*.

- Genesis 6:7 describes God as having regrets that he ever made human beings due to the great sin of the human race. The plain meaning of the text entails that God can undertake a course of action and then have regrets if matters don't turn out as he'd hoped.

- In Genesis 18:21 God says he will go down to Sodom to see whether their sin is as egregious as he has been hearing.

The plain sense suggests both that God exists in physical space at a higher elevation than Sodom and thus that he must descend through space to get there. It also entails that God didn't have perfect knowledge at the time of what was happening and thus he needed to learn.

Together, these four scriptures seem to give us a plain sense (at least for an average contemporary English reader) that God learns, he changes his mind, he has regrets, and he is unaware of what is happening in parts of the world such that he needs to travel to them to find out. I ask you: do you want to leave your theology there? Does the plain sense of those narrative descriptions determine the parameters of your theological thinking?

Some theologians have answered that with a "yes" at least for some of these cases. For example, open theists have embraced various limitations in the divine nature based, at least in part, on what they believe to be the plain meaning of these passages. But other theologians, and this other group constitutes the significant majority, have instead insisted that a proper theology of God requires us to go beyond these "plain" meanings. For example, a theology known as classical theism has dominated the Christian tradition and classical theists interpret God as having a set of attributes including perfect omniscience, omnipotence, omnipresence, immutability, impassibility, and atemporal eternity, attributes that together *require* that the theologian find a meaning beyond the apparent plain sense. From within this theological framework, it is standard to interpret these passages as idiomatic including anthropomorphism (describing God in human form) and anthropopathism (describing God with human emotion).

This brings us back to the point that moving beyond the plain sense in constructing a theological understanding of God and his relationship to us is part and parcel of Christian theology: it's *what we do as Christians*. When progressive

Christians move beyond the plain sense in their own wrestling with scripture in order to make sense of issues like natural science and ethical understanding, they are simply engaged in that same time-honored enterprise.

Childers writes that in the progressive pastor's class, "The Bible was presented as morally dubious in parts, and the only option offered was to reject or reinterpret the sections that didn't resonate."[171] She says this as if it is a *bad* thing. And she certainly tries to make it sound bad with the trivializing description "didn't resonate." But it isn't just that passages that commend beating children (Proverbs 22:15) or the genocidal slaughter of women, children, and the elderly (Joshua 6:21) don't "resonate" with the reader: it's that these actions seem to be false and harmful, if not outright evil. And thus, these examples provide an excellent reason for the Christian to move beyond the plain meaning of the text.

Wrestling and Fear

Time and again, Childers condemns the character of those with whom she disagrees. One of her go-to strategies is to charge them with irreverence. For example, she writes "One afternoon, I became distressed about what seemed like a profound disregard for the fear of God among my classmates . . . ."[172] Folks like Childers tend to get suspicious when Christians ask hard questions of the text. The critical point to keep in mind is that to the extent that there *is* irreverent disregard present, it need not be irreverence toward *God;* rather, it may merely be irreverence toward your problematic theology of God. To be sure, if you can't even tell the difference between the Bible and your *interpretation* of the Bible or God and your theology of God then it is not surprising that you will mistakenly interpret such reading as opposition to God.

---

171 Childers, *Another Gospel?* 57.

172 Childers, *Another Gospel?* 102.

One more thing: we should also emphasize that the entire process of questioning and considering where we need to move beyond a plain sense of the text is not irreverent at all. Quite the contrary, in fact: the willingness to ask hard questions is evidence of *reverent engagement*. The truth is that the closer your relationship is with a person, the more willing you are to broach difficult subjects with that person. If you hardly know your boss, you will avoid difficult conversations and awkward topics. But if you have known your boss intimately for twenty years, you will confidently stride into her office and launch right into the unmentionable topic. Those with a superficial relationship with the boss may interpret that as irreverence, but the situation is, in fact, the opposite.

And that is precisely what we find in Scripture. From Abraham questioning the destruction of Sodom to Moses reminding God not to abandon his covenant with Israel to the Psalmist pleading for mercy to Job demanding an account for his suffering to Jacob himself who received the name "Israel" because he wrestled with God through the night, time and again, those who are closest to God are those who were willing to argue with God, challenge God, and ask hard questions of God. When we willingly enter into that same process of theological reflection on the most difficult and daunting of topics, we express and embody our own willingness to wrestle with God as those grafted into Israel. Consequently, that which Childers describes as "a profound disregard for the fear of God" looks to me rather like a profound and moving embodiment of what it means to be true Israel, the willingness to ask hard questions and wrestle with God as Jacob wrestled with the angel.

8

The Atonement
is Not Penal Substitution

Childers claims that progressive Christians reject the message of Jesus in favor of "another" gospel. Her case begins
with the course with the progressive pastor. As she describes
it, the pastor and students together began questioning the very
heart of the Gospel in the atoning work of Christ. Eventually,
that questioning turned into outright rejection:

> Several of my fellow students were beginning to rethink the
> Cross. They were questioning the whole "Jesus died to pay
> for my sins" concept because they believed it implicated the
> character of God. If the Father required a blood sacrifice to
> atone for sin, it made him like a capricious pagan deity. If he
> desired that this sacrifice be made by his only Son, it made
> him something even worse: a cosmic child abuser.
>
> Historically, Christians have believed that Jesus died for
> our sins . . . in our place . . . as our substitute.[173]

---

173 Childers, *Another Gospel?* 84. Cf. 86

Thus, Childers believes that these progressives have outright rejected the very *raison d'etre* of Christianity in the atoning work of Christ.

Childers begins by identifying several factors of concern that people have raised against the *penal substitutionary theory of atonement* including the concern that it presents God as akin to a pagan deity who needs a blood sacrifice to placate his wrath and that it turns him into a "cosmic child abuser" by having his son play that role. Next, she then claims that those objections (which are clearly specific to the penal substitutionary theory of atonement) are, in fact, objections to the Christian *doctrine* of atonement. The confusion is evident in the passage quoted above when she concludes that those who reject penal substitutionary theory thereby also reject *any* notion of substitutionary atonement. Thus, Childers assumes that the substitutionary atonement just is the same thing as the *penal substitutionary theoretical interpretation*. It isn't.

Allow me to illustrate the nature of the confusion. When I was a little kid, I told people I hated cheese. It turns out that I was mistaken. In my youthful naivete, the only cheese I knew of was Kraft processed cheese slices (aka Kraft Singles). Alas, I didn't know about Applewood cheddar or Monterey Jack or Gouda or Parmigiano. As a result, I had conflated the token (Kraft singles) with the type of thing (cheese) and thereby dismissed the latter because I did not like the former.

Just as it would be a gross error to reject all cheese because you don't like Kraft Singles, so it would be a gross error to conclude that someone else must reject all cheese the moment they say they don't like Kraft Singles. To the progressive Christian who raises concerns like those noted above, the penal substitutionary theory of atonement is equivalent to Kraft Singles. They don't like it at all. That doesn't mean, however, that they reject the doctrine of substitutionary atonement. The truth is that there are *many* theories of atonement and the Christian who rejects a specific theory like penal substitution does not thereby reject the atonement. Nor need that individual endorse any other specific theory to accept the doctrine of atonement. Remember that Christianity is founded on Christ and not our doctrinal theories about him or what he accomplished.

In this chapter I want to do the following: first, we will discuss the doctrine of atonement and distinguish it more fully from theories of atonement. Next, we will introduce the penal substitutionary theory of atonement, discuss its place in Christian history, and note some of the objections to it so we can at least have a better sense of what concerns many progressive Christians. Finally, we will conclude the chapter by returning to the evidence that Childers has conflated objections to the penal substitutionary theory of atonement with objections to the atonement simpliciter.

Theories, Atonement, and Atonement Theories

To begin with, we need to clarify the concept of a theory and its relationship to the doctrine(s) it seeks to explain. Unfortunately, misunderstanding is common among Christian conservatives as regards the nature and function of theories. For example, I have heard many conservative Christians say that "Evolution is only a theory." The qualification "only" suggests that the word "theory" is here being interpreted to mean something equivalent to *speculative conjecture* as with that guy who says, "So I got this *theory* about how the Chinese government created COVID19." In that case, you can bet that what follows will be a heady dose of very speculative conjecture. But this is *not* what is meant when we say evolution is a theory, for evolution isn't mere conjecture. Rather, it is supported by multiple lines of independent evidence.[174] Instead, evolution

---

174 It is a safe bet that Childers believes Neo-Darwinian evolution is closer to speculative conjecture given that she opposes "Darwinian evolution" with what she calls "the biblical account," *Another Gospel?* 78. That said, always beware of people who say "the biblical account" when what they really should say is "my interpretation of the Bible." For an account of how to reconcile evolution and

is a theory in the sense that *it is an explanatory framework for multiple data points.*

For the concept of a theory as an explanatory framework, my go-to example is the theory of plate tectonics. This is a geological theory developed in the 1960s to explain a range of geological features including volcanos, sea floor spreading, earthquakes, mountain ranges, and the suggestive fit between South America and Africa. According to the theory, the surface of the earth is made up of a collection of vast fractured plates that rub against one another, crash into each other, and pull apart. And those various phenomena produce all the above-mentioned geological features and more. Plate tectonics is a theory, but it is not "only" a theory. Rather, it is an excellent theory and as such it provides a powerful explanatory framework for all these data points. Indeed, it has been so successful that it has cleared the field of any viable competitors.

Just as scientists propose theories to explain datapoints in nature, so Christian systematic theologians propose theories in order to explain various datapoints in theology. One field of systematic theological inquiry concerns the question of atonement, or how God heals the breach of the fall so that human beings (and indeed the totality of creation) are made *at one* with God the Father. The end goal of an atonement theory was captured in the title to a famous monograph by medieval theologian Anselm: *Cur Deus Homo? (Why the God-Man?).* In other words, an atonement theory seeks to explain why God the Son incarnated into the world as Jesus Christ, grew up and walked amongst us for thirty plus years, died on a cross, and resurrected. What was the *point* of that whole story? How does it work? What was God doing? That's what the theory seeks to explain.

Atonement doctrine provides multiple initial statements which constitute part of the total set of data to be explained.

Christianity, see the work of the evangelical Christian organization Biologos: https://biologos.org/

For example, God the Father sent his Son out of *love for the world* (John 3:16), the Son *became a curse for us* (Galatians 3:13) thereby *reconciling the world to himself* (2 Corinthians 5:19), including *all things* (not just human beings) (Colossians 1:20). Biblical descriptions like these provide datapoints that the Christian theologian seeks to explain by the construction of an atonement theory.

The doctrine of atonement is obviously at the very heart of Christian identity and proclamation. Christians exist because of the Good News, and we seek to proclaim it to the world. But it is one thing to recognize that God has acted in Christ and the result is the promise of the reconciliation of all things. It is quite another to offer a theory (i.e. an overarching explanatory framework) of why Jesus incarnated, lived a perfect life, died, and resurrected in a manner that realized at-one-ment between God and a fallen and sinful creation. An explanation for all these facts brings us into the sphere of atonement theory equivalent to plate tectonics' explanation of the origin of volcanos, sea floor spreading, earthquakes, mountain ranges, and the fit of continents.

In contrast to plate tectonics, the field of atonement theories has not been dominated by one view. Rather, theologians have proposed many atonement theories over the centuries and several remain in contention. I use the book *The Nature of the Atonement: Four Views* as a textbook in one of my systematic theology seminary classes.[175] The book features four theologians, each defending a specific theory of atonement in debate with the others. Greg Boyd defends a Christus Victor theory, Bruce Reichenbach advocates for a healing theory, and Thomas Schreiner champions the penal substitutionary theory. Though opinions will predictably differ on which theory is strongest, they are all perfectly legitimate (and thus orthodox) ways to interpret the biblical data of atonement.

---

175 James Beilby and Paul R. Eddy, eds., *The Nature of the Atonement: Four Views* (IVP Academic, 2006).

Nor does *The Nature of the Atonement* exhaust the options. Indeed, far from it: there are *many* other theories that are still debated today including the recapitulation theory, the moral influence theory, the ransom theory, the satisfaction theory, the Girardean theory, and the governmental theory. I don't claim that each of these theories is equally strong or that each one is as consistent with the orthodox Christian tradition as every other. The point is simply to underscore that the field of theology is full of theoretical interpretations of atonement. And no one theoretical interpretation is a requirement of mainstream Christian orthodoxy. Christians are required by confession to accept the doctrine of atonement, but they are not required to accept any one theory of atonement and that includes the penal substitutionary theory.

I said that *The Nature of the Atonement* includes *four* theologians as contributors, but I only mentioned three theories. The fourth proposal is something of an outlier. In his essay, Joel Green bypasses the project of theory articulation and defense altogether, instead proposing that we think about these various accounts of atonement not as mutually exclusive theories but rather as mutually enriching metaphors. As a root metaphor to organize the field, Green argues that we should think of these various images in terms of a *kaleidoscope*: just as the turn of the kaleidoscope reveals endless new insights through the refraction of light, so "turning" the doctrine of atonement through the refracting light of various metaphors provides endless new insights into the theology of atonement. In other words, maybe we don't need a theory at all; maybe, we're better served simply with a plurality of metaphors.

At the very least, Green's essay reminds us that we don't *need* to have a theory of the atonement. Think about romantic love for a moment: it is one thing to *experience* love, but it is quite another to have a *workable theory* of love. For example, I once read about a biochemical theory that seeks to define love wholly in terms of oxytocin's effect on the brain. According to the theory, love is just a chemical reaction. I couldn't help but wonder if the researchers proposing the theory really believed that their love for their children and spouses was, in fact, nothing more than biochemical reactions in the brain. I don't buy that for a minute. If that were the only theory of love on offer then I'd definitely prefer to stick with a plurality of metaphors about love: better not to have a theory at all than to settle for a really bad one.

The same is true of the atonement. It is one thing to believe in the atonement, experience the atonement, and benefit from the atonement: it is quite another to have a satisfactory *theory of* the atonement. So while you could embrace a specific theory of the atonement, you may conclude that all the theories on offer are unsatisfactory. In that case, you might instead resonate with Green's *kaleidoscope* view and thereby conclude that we are best served thinking of atonement in terms of a catalogue of mutually enriching metaphors.

The great historian of doctrine Jaroslav Pelikan succinctly summarizes the plurality of perspective available to the Christian as follows: "As in the New Testament . . . so in the tradition of the church there were many figures of speech—not at all seen as mutually exclusive, but as complementary—to represent the atonement effected by the life, death, and resurrection of Christ."[176] In other words, Scripture and the church have always recognized an abundance of images or metaphors to describe the reconciling work of Christ.

Underlying all these images, we have the second section of the Apostles' Creed. This passage beautifully summarizes the core substructure of Christian confession as regards Christ and his work:

---

176 Pelikan, *The Melody of Theology: A Philosophical Dictionary* (Harvard University Press, 1988), 12. C.S. Lewis observed, "The central Christian belief is that Christ's death has somehow put us right with God and given us a fresh start. Theories as to how it did this are another matter. A good many different theories have been held as to how it works; what all Christians are agreed on is that it does work." *Mere Christianity* (HarperOne, 2000), 55.

> I believe in Jesus Christ, his only Son, our Lord,
> who was conceived by the Holy Spirit
> and born of the virgin Mary.
> He suffered under Pontius Pilate,
> was crucified, died, and was buried;
> he descended to hell.
> The third day he rose again from the dead.
> He ascended to heaven
> and is seated at the right hand of God the Father almighty.
> From there he will come to judge the living and the dead.

The Creed lists a series of actions undertaken by Jesus including conception, birth, suffering, crucifixion, death, descent into hell, resurrection, ascension, session, and the second coming and judgment. That is a capsule summary of the Gospel proclamation.

But what the creed does not require of people is a specific theory to explain that collection of doctrines. As Pelikan puts it, no one specific interpretation of the atonement ever gained "the status of a dogma of the universal church, whose only ecumenical statement of faith, the Nicene Creed, contented itself with saying that the life, death, and resurrection had been 'for' humanity, *without specifying how and why*."[177] Jesus promised the Holy Spirit would lead the church into truth, but clearly that truth did not include unanimity on how the atonement works.

In our opening section, we noted that Childers says that "Historically, Christians have believed that Jesus died for our sins . . . in our place . . . as our substitute." While Childers is right to recognize the centrality of substitution in the doctrine of atonement, she makes a deep error when she confuses this with the concept of *penal substitution* which is not an element in other theories and most certainly is not required in order to embrace, experience, or benefit from the atonement.

---

177 Pelikan, *The Melody of Theology,* 14, emphasis added.

Putting a Spotlight on Penal Substitutionary Theory

Now that we have a better understanding of the relationship between doctrine and theory and of the nature of penal substitution as a theory, we should devote some effort to understanding a bit more about the debate concerning the theory. As we have seen, critics claim (among other things) that the theory presents God as a pagan deity requiring blood sacrifice to appease his wrath "like a capricious pagan deity" and perhaps even a "cosmic child abuser." As bad as that sounds, some critics of penal substitution take the charges to the next level. For example, Orthodox theologian Brad Jersak contends that penal substitutionary theory constitutes *heresy* because it pits the Father against the Son, thereby creating a fracture in the triune life of God.[178]

There is a vast literature debating the biblical, moral, historical, theological, and pastoral controversies created by penal substitutionary theory. But to be frank, that is a rabbit trail down which we best not go. My concern is less with drawing a final conclusion concerning the legitimacy of the criticisms than simply getting us to recognize that *people who reject penal substitution as a theory may still be Christians in good standing because Christianity, as such, does not require acceptance of penal substitution.* In other words, I am not interested in arguing that you should reject penal substitution (but I won't be sad if you do).

We can underscore the point by noting the extent to which there is a serious debate about the historical origins of penal substitution. So, when did the penal substitutionary theory begin? Not surprisingly, it depends on whom you ask. Proponents not uncommonly argue that it is present in the Bible and is the root proclamation of the Christian tradition.[179] However,

---

178 See *A More Christlike God, A More Beautiful Gospel* (CWR Press, 2015), 278-9.

179 See, for example, Steve Jeffery, Michael Ovey, and Andrew Sach, *Pierced*

it should be noted that there is some ambiguity as people who trace the theory to the Patristic era often blur the line between pre-theoretic *anticipations* of penal substitutionary theory (e.g. metaphors of sacrifice and satisfaction) and the formal articulation of the theory as such.

Other theologians date the theory's origin to centuries later. One common view among historical theologians traces penal substitutionary theory to the sixteenth century Reformers, particularly John Calvin, as representing a further development of Anselm's medieval satisfaction theory of atonement. Consider, for example, how Ben Pugh describes penal substitution:

> We look now at the time-honored and venerable evangelical doctrine of penal substitution. The term is attributed to nineteenth-century Princeton theologian, Charles Hodge, though the concept was birthed during the Reformation. It has become the most widely held doctrine amongst evangelicals. Penal substitution simply means that Jesus died to bear the penalty for my sins, hence 'penal,' and that he did this in my place, hence 'substitution.' The bearing of penalty implies that God needed to punish sin and that something actually happened to Jesus on the cross that constituted a punishment of the innocent Christ and which was accepted by the Father as a satisfactory equivalent to the punishment that was due to the human race as a whole.[180]

Pugh's location of the origins of penal substitutionary theory (which he refers to as a 'doctrine') in the Reformation is a common view. Needless to say, it is even more problematic for Childers to insist that assent to a theory is a requirement of orthodox Christian confession when that theory itself does

---

for Our Transgressions: Rediscovering the Glory of Penal Substitution (Crossway, 2007).

180 Pugh, *Atonement Theories: A Way Through the Maze* (Cascade, 2014), 63.

not clearly appear in the theological record until *1500 years after the time of Christ.*

One point that is particularly helpful in Pugh's comments is how he observes that penal substitutionary theory is the most popular view of atonement among evangelicals. When one lacks familiarity with theological perspectives outside one's own tradition (as oft occurs in evangelicalism), it is all too common to make the error of assuming that one's own tradition just is the same thing as Christian orthodoxy as such. And that appears to be precisely the mistake that Childers makes here. Indeed, her lack of familiarity with historical theology is evident in the fact that she criticizes Brian Zahnd for saying that penal substitutionary atonement originated with Calvin, with no apparent awareness that Zahnd is just endorsing a standard view.[181]

To sum up, whether you want to identify penal substitutionary theory as originating in John Calvin, the Patristics, or Paul the Apostle, the fact remains that *the Christian tradition has never required a theory of atonement as part of the dogmas of essential confession.* Consequently, to accuse Christians who reject penal substitutionary theory of rejecting the atonement itself is a dangerous and deeply damaging mistake, one which effectively slanders fellow Christians as presenting "another" gospel when they have done nothing of the kind.

Final Thoughts on Atonement Confusion

To conclude this chapter, I will highlight some additional examples from the book to drive home the point that the passage with which we began the chapter is not an outlier or a momentary lapse into confusion. On the contrary, it represents a much wider, indeed, systemic confusion in Childers' understanding of the atonement, one that is all-too-common in the provincial precincts of evangelicalism.

---

181 Childers, *Another Gospel?* 209.

In her chapter on atonement, Childers unpacks the early Pauline confession that Jesus died for our sins in 1 Corinthians 15:3 as follows:

> It means that Jesus died in our place . . . as our substitute. But the Bible tells us that Jesus also paid the penalty for our sin, which adds a deeper element to our understanding. This is called penal substitutionary atonement. The word *penal* has to do with punishment and penalty. Of all the biblical descriptions of atonement, this is the one most commonly rejected by progressive Christians.[182]

In this passage, Childers states that she believes Paul is endorsing penal substitutionary atonement in 1 Corinthians 15:3-*ff.* I don't have a problem with that as such: she's welcome to her opinions. And it is not uncommon for defenders of a specific theory to insist that their view is already present (in at least protean form) in the biblical documents themselves.

The problem arises, rather, in the fact that Childers goes on to insist that this theoretical interpretation of atonement is both *the one way* to understand atonement throughout Scripture and *the one view that has been taught throughout the history of the church*. She writes: "This belief has united Christians throughout the ages and across cultures and continents. It's the story Scripture tells from the fall of Eden in Genesis to its restoration in Revelation."[183] As a result, when her progressive pastor questions penal substitution, Childers renders a stark judgment: "He stripped the Cross of the Atonement . . . ."[184] Suffice it to say, he did nothing of the kind.

Later, Childers claims that William Paul Young "denies the substitutionary atonement of Jesus" in his book *Lies We*

182 Childers, *Another Gospel?* 204.

183 Childers, *Another Gospel?* 205.

184 Childers, *Another Gospel?* 203.

Believe About God.[185] However, in that very book Young writes of Christ: "He himself is the atoning sacrifice for our sins, and not only for ours, but also for those of the *whole* world (1 John 2:2 Berean Study Bible, emphasis mine)."[186] In fact, Childers' quote from Young makes clear that his real target is penal substitution given that he criticizes the notion that "God required child sacrifice to appease a sense of righteous indignation and the fury of holiness . . . ."[187] So there is no question but that Young's target is this specific theory. When the contradiction between what Young says and what Childers claims he says is this direct, you really have two choices: either Childers is *lying* about Young, or she is simply confused in her basic understanding of what the atonement is. I believe the evidence supports the latter conclusion: like so many evangelicals, she is simply unaware that her preferred theory is but one theoretical interpretation among many in the history of the church.

The same bald misunderstanding repeats itself throughout the chapter as Childers quickly works her way through a number of progressive Christians including Steve Chalke, Rob Bell, Brian Zahnd, Richard Rohr, and Rachel Held Evans.[188] In each case, Childers accuses the individual of rejecting the Gospel of Christ's atoning work when, in fact, each of her interlocutors is simply directing criticisms toward the *penal substitutionary theory* of atonement.

Near the end of the chapter, after presenting a defense of penal substitution, Childers reiterates her absolutely outrageous claim that this particular theory has been endorsed by a unanimous witness of the Christian tradition throughout history: "These are some of the many reasons that Christians, for two thousand years, have affirmed that Jesus died for our

185 Childers, *Another Gospel?* 207.

186 *Lies We Believe About God* (Atria, 2018), 248.

187 Cited in Childers, *Another Gospel?* 208.

188 Childers, *Another Gospel?* 209-212.

sins."[189] For the umpteenth time, believing that "Jesus died for our sins" is just not the same thing as believing the penal substitutionary theory that Jesus Christ died as a blood sacrifice with our sin imputed to him to absorb the wrath of the Father against sin.

All of this slander against fellow Christians is bad enough. But Childers then caps it off by ending the chapter with a final, truly reprehensible rhetorical assault on all Christians who dare to reject her theory of atonement:

> They are simply constructing a codependent and impotent god who is powerless to stop evil. That god is not really good. That god is not the God of the Bible.
> That god cannot save you.[190]

It is crucial that we appreciate the full gravity of what Childers is saying here. If you reject her penal substitutionary theory, she insists that you are left with another god (note the lowercase 'g'), one who is impotent, not good, unable to save, and certainly not the God of the Bible. These are completely absurd and deeply incendiary charges. And by making them, Childers effectively damns the vast swathe of Christianity that has never endorsed the penal substitutionary theory. How ironic that one should engage in such a crass effort to divide the church and malign fellow Christians, and to do it all ostensibly in the name of a doctrine of *at-one-ment*.

189 Childers, *Another Gospel?* 223.
190 Childers, *Another Gospel?* 224.

9

Final Judgment
is Not Eternal Conscious Torment

Chapter 10 of *Another Gospel?* takes aim at progressive views on the doctrine of hell. However, before Childers turns her sights on progressive Christians, she first provides a shocking glimpse into her own upbringing beginning with a Sunday school teacher who traumatized a seven-year-old Alisa with threats that children who did not accept Jesus as their savior would be "on fire in hell forever while worms slowly eat your flesh for all eternity." Nor was this spiritual abuse a one-off event: Childers recalls that this woman often terrified her poor Sunday school students with the most lurid threats of hell. Indeed, she even carried her campaign of terror into the local Christian elementary school.[191] As you can imagine, this abusive conduct left deep scars on Childers which is probably why she bothers to mention it some forty years later.

Nor was it just hell that caused stress to a young Alisa. Her fears were compounded by another doctrine, the secret rapture. That curious doctrine, which is a unique feature of

---

191 Childers, *Another Gospel?* 177.

Christian dispensationalism, claims that prior to Jesus' public second coming there will be a secret second coming in which he will whisk his faithful believers away prior to pouring out judgment upon the earth. Many conservative evangelicals are taught this idiosyncratic teaching as if it were just the church's historic teaching on the second coming of Jesus. It isn't. Rather, as I noted in chapter 1, it is an idiosyncratic feature of the dispensationalist system.

Although the rapture was purportedly "good news", it left Childers "living in almost constant existential crisis . . . ." Things got so bad that she recalls, "I began to realize that my main fear wasn't simply the concepts of heaven or hell. *It was eternity*. I was absolutely petrified of living forever . . . no matter where I ended up."[192] Childers adds soberly, "As the years went on, this fear and panic became my new normal."[193] I appreciate Childers' candor and vulnerability in sharing that experience. But what she is expressing here are some practical reasons why so many Christians, and not just "progressives," are deeply critical of the teachings about the afterlife that are popular in conservative evangelicalism, as well as the very dubious wisdom by which those doctrines are often shared with children. In this penultimate chapter, we turn our attention to Childers' teaching on hell.

Rob Bell on Hell

Not surprisingly, Childers begins her survey of the errors of progressive thinking about hell with Rob Bell's book *Love Wins*. This is the Bell quote she gives us:

> A staggering number of people have been taught that a select few Christians will spend forever in a peaceful, joyous place called heaven, while the rest of humanity spends forever in

192 Childers, *Another Gospel?* 178.
193 Childers, *Another Gospel?* 178-9.

torment and punishment in hell with no chance for anything better. It's been clearly communicated to many that this belief is a central truth of the Christian faith and to reject it is in essence, to reject Jesus. This is misguided and toxic and ultimately subverts the contagious spread of Jesus's message of love, peace, forgiveness, and joy that our world desperately needs to hear.[194]

Childers concludes from this passage that Bell "claims that hell is at odds with Jesus' teaching."[195] But that's not true at all. Bell never claims that *hell* per se is opposed to Jesus' teaching. The matter, rather, concerns *what kind of hell one is teaching*. Once again, Childers confuses the token (i.e. a critique of a particular *theory* of hell) with the type (i.e. the doctrine of hell itself). We can summarize the views Bell is targeting in terms of three distinct theses:

- *Pessimism Thesis:* There will be many more people who are lost than are saved.
- *Eternal Conscious Torment Thesis:* Those who are lost will spend forever in torment.
- *Dogma Thesis:* Failure to accept the Pessimism Thesis and/ or the Eternal Conscious Torment Thesis is equivalent to rejecting Jesus himself.

Christians who endorse the pessimism thesis often appeal to Matthew 7:14: "But small is the gate and narrow the road that leads to life, and only a few find it." However, I think that is missing the point: Jesus is not concerned here to provide a final snapshot of the ultimate ratio of saved-to-lost; his point, rather, is to exhort people to repent. What is more, many other biblical passages are much more optimistic about the numbers of the

---

194 Cited in Childers, *Another Gospel?* 184.

195 Childers, *Another Gospel?* 184.

saved (e.g. Revelation 7:9-10). So it is a curious thing indeed to *require* Christians to be pessimists about such matters.

What about the eternal conscious torment thesis? There are several biblical passages that have been interpreted in support of this doctrine (e.g. Matthew 25:41, 46; Revelation 14:9-11; Revelation 20:10). And this view is indeed the most widely held theory of posthumous judgment in the history of the Christian church.

That said, just as Christian orthodoxy has never required a specific theory of atonement as part of the doctrine of atonement, so it has never required a specific theory of posthumous punishment (i.e. the punishment of those outside Christ following the general resurrection) as part of the doctrine of posthumous punishment. Just as the major Christian creeds do not endorse a specific theory of atonement, so they do not endorse specific theories of posthumous punishment. The Apostles' Creed confesses only this about the afterlife: "the resurrection of the body, and the life everlasting." Similarly, the Nicene Creed confesses only this: "We look forward to the resurrection of the dead, and to life in the world to come."

While there are many theories of atonement, there are only three major theories of posthumous judgment in the Christian tradition: the above-mentioned eternal conscious torment view as well as annihilationism, and universalism. According to annihilationism, those who are outside Christ are resurrected to a judgment that results ultimately in the cessation of their existence. According to universalism, those who are outside Christ are resurrected to a judgment that results ultimately in their reconciliation to the Father in Christ. All three views appeal to their own set of supporting biblical texts and all three views claim theological support back to the Patristic era. For example, Irenaeus and Arnobius have both been identified as early annihilationists while Origen and Gregory of Nyssa were both universalists.[196] And as I noted earlier, Gregory was also one of the formulators of the Nicene Creed.

As with atonement, my concern is not to defend a specific view of posthumous judgment but rather simply to point out that *alternatives to eternal conscious torment have always been part of the conversation of Christian orthodoxy.* Thus, Rob Bell is absolutely right to reject the Dogma Thesis. Even if you think we ought to be pessimistic about the number of saved and to believe that the lost will suffer in hell forever, nonetheless, it doesn't follow that other Christians are *required* to agree with you in order to be saved. For a very good introductory survey of the various biblical, theological, and philosophical arguments for eternal conscious torment, annihilationism, and universalism, I recommend the Zondervan book *Four Views on Hell.*[197]

In contrast to her penchant for making sweeping historical judgments regarding the alleged consensus in favor of penal substitutionary theory of atonement, Childers admits that universalism has been endorsed by Christians throughout church history. (Childers does not specifically acknowledge the third view, annihilationism.[198]) However, she insists that the view that all people will eventually be reconciled through Christ is "heretical."[199] She concludes that this view "is not biblical, nor does it represent the historic witness of the church."[200]

As per her usual, Childers conflates "not biblical" with "not my interpretation of the Bible." As for the fact that universalism

---

196 For an overview of some of the complexities with interpreting Irenaeus' eschatology on this point see Thomas D. McGlothlin, *Resurrection as Salvation: Development and Conflict in Pre-Nicene Paulinism* (Cambridge University Press, 2018), 88-89.

197 Sprinkle, Preston, ed., *Four Views on Hell,* 2nd ed. (Zondervan, 2016).

198 Childers does quote Richard Bauckham who makes a passing reference to annihilationism. See *Another Gospel?* 187.

199 Childers, *Another Gospel?* 186.

200 Childers, *Another Gospel?* 187.

does not represent the "historical witness of the church," she is right if historical witness is taken to mean the most commonly held view throughout history. But of course, being a minority position is not the same thing as being *heretical*. After all, as I noted above, the doctrine of secret rapture that Childers embraced as a child is most definitely a highly idiosyncratic minority view. However, that doesn't automatically qualify it as heretical. So what other reason does Childers offer to call universalism heresy?

Beyond her appeal to majority historical opinion, Childers' main argument for the view that universalism is heretical appears to consist in providing arguments for eternal conscious torment. Thus, she refers to Matthew 25:46 where Jesus says, "The sheep find eternal life while the goats are condemned to 'eternal punishment.'"[201] She then concludes:

> These words were some of the final recorded teachings of Jesus before his arrest and crucifixion. He wanted his followers to know that there would be a final judgment. There would be eternal life and eternal punishment. The door to his Kingdom would one day close. He urges us to be ready. Despite the progressive Christian attempt to soften or reinterpret these teachings, I couldn't shake the power of Jesus' words.[202]

However, the fact that there are some verses which one can interpret in support of eternal conscious torment *does not* entail that the alternative views are suddenly heresies. Indeed, as the *Four Views on Hell* book makes clear, there is a solid biblical, theological, and philosophical case to be made for each theory. Rather than accuse Christians like Bell of rejecting the doctrine of hell or espousing heresy, Childers should, at the very least, have applauded the point that Christian orthodoxy does not require either pessimism about the extent of salvation

---

201 Childers, *Another Gospel?* 192.

202 Childers, *Another Gospel?* 192-3.

or acceptance of the eternal conscious torment theory of hell. On those matters, at least, Bell is surely correct.

Hell as Eternal Torture

Childers succinctly summarizes the nature of posthumous judgment as follows: "First, hell is eternal. Second, in hell souls are conscious. Third, hell is torment."[203] There is no shortage of irony that Childers is so adamant about retaining the doctrine of eternal conscious torment in her understanding of Christianity given that it caused such, er, torment in her youth. At this point, I think it would be worthwhile to take a closer look at the eternal conscious torment view of hell in order to understand better why many other Christians like Bell are strongly opposed to it.

To begin with, we need to understand that the infliction of severe mental, emotional, and/or physical suffering on another person for punitive means is, by definition, *torture*. Thus, if God sends people to hell as a form of eternal *punishment*, as Childers clearly affirms, then he is consigning them to an eternity of *torture*. Thus, Childers' view of posthumous judgment entails that God eternally tortures the vast majority of human beings. I would think that right there is a rather bitter theological pill to swallow.

Second, we need to understand the intensity of the torture to which these poor creatures will be subjected. It is standard in Christian theology to recognize that suffering on the eternal conscious torment view of hell is greater than any suffering one can imagine.[204] So when you learn of the most horrendous examples of physical, emotional, and/or mental suffering of other people in this mortal coil, and you find yourself sickened and stunned by the degree to which people can be subjected

---

203 Childers, *Another Gospel?* 193.

204 C.S. Lewis' attempt in *The Great Divorce* to present hell as a dreary sojourn in a rainy British Midlands city is definitely the outlier.

to such suffering, remember that the torture awaiting those in hell is much, much worse. And it goes on . . . forever.

Third, Christians who defend eternal conscious torment disagree about whether God inflicts the punishment or whether God allows individuals to punish themselves through self-imposed suffering. C.S. Lewis famously argued the latter position, for example, in the apparent belief that it is more humane than God actively torturing people forever. However, I think the improvement is negligible: even if the torture is self-inflicted, it is still *appropriated by God as punishment*, the very means by which he inflicts never-ending punitive anguish on creatures.

Fourth, Christians need to think about how eternal conscious torment relates to heaven. Imagine, for a moment, that you go to heaven and your beloved daughter goes to hell where she will be subjected to unimaginable suffering in body and soul forever. When you are fully conformed to the image of God's Son (Romans 8:29) how could you experience unimaginable bliss even as your daughter is being endlessly tortured?

This is a huge problem for the eternal conscious torment view and theologians have proposed two primary responses.[205] The first solution is to say that God's resurrected people in heaven will experience unimaginable bliss because God blinds them to the torture of their beloved family and friends in hell. On this view, God will mercifully keep you from seeing the roasting flesh and hearing the tortured screams of your beloved child. And that delusion is just what is required to ensure that heaven remains heaven.

I do not find that to be a very satisfying view to put it mildly. Indeed, it seems to me that it is equivalent to saying that you can enjoy your vacation at the luxury resort bordering a poverty-stricken slum only because the walls are high enough to block out the misery and cries of the dying on the other side. This seems to turn the new heavens and new earth into a sham.

---

205 In my book *Faith Lacking Understanding: Theology through a glass, darkly* (Paternoster, 2008), chapter 7, I survey a total of four possibilities.

And it definitely seems out of step with Paul's teaching that when completeness comes the imperfect disappears, we shall see face to face and be known fully (1 Corinthians 13:10, 12). How can we see face to face and be fully known if our joy is dependent on God blinding us to the torment of our loved ones?

This leads us to the second major solution, one that has been embraced by theologians from Tertullian to Thomas Aquinas to John Piper. This account really takes the bull by the horns by insisting that the suffering of those being tortured in hell will be a cause of *delight and praise* for God's people because it manifests his justice visited upon those poor wretches even as it also magnifies the nature of his grace extended to the elect. Just as the saints of Revelation long for their blood to be avenged (Revelation 6:10) and praise God when Babylon falls (Revelation 18:1-3), so we long for the blood of the righteous to be avenged. And we will praise God for eternity as we drink in the spectacle of the damned: those that we once considered mothers and fathers, sisters and brothers, wives and husbands, daughters and sons, friends, and acquaintances, being tortured forever, praise be to his name!

Um, *yeah*. . . . the view that those in heaven will delight in the judgment of the damned may have the virtue of consistency, but in my view its virtues stop there. To propose that becoming fully like Christ means being able to take delight in the torture of my daughter does not strike me as a lofty glorying in the sovereign majesty of God. Nor does it look like an admirable hatred of sin. On the contrary, it strikes me as a base perversion of holiness, one that distorts conformity to Christ into something truly dark and unrecognizable. Of course, you are more than welcome to disagree with me on that point: rest assured, I won't revoke your Christian credentials for doing so! All I ask is that you please extend the same courtesy back to the many Christians who will disagree with you and the eternal conscious torment theory.

Childers and the General Resurrection

Before we leave all this unpleasantness behind, we should return to Childers' summary of her views of hell for one more go. As we saw, she summarizes her views like this: "First, hell is eternal. Second, in hell souls are conscious. Third, hell is torment." Note that Childers refers here not to persons but rather to *souls* being conscious in hell. This implies a picture where those outside Christ die and then go to hell where their souls are tortured forever, full stop.

But that is not orthodox Christianity.

Orthodox Christianity affirms the general resurrection both of the righteous and the unrighteous (e.g. Daniel 12:2; John 5:25, 28-9). What this means for those in hell is that they suffer not simply as disembodied souls but as resurrected *persons*. Where the doctrine of eternal conscious torment is concerned, this means that they are resurrected to be tortured forever both in body (the pains of sense) and soul (the pains of loss). However, Childers makes no reference of the general resurrection to judgment, instead only referring to conscious souls.

We should consider a charitable interpretation of her words. Perhaps Childers is treating the term "soul" as a synecdoche (i.e. a literary device that treats the part of something as the whole). In this case, she would be treating the part (soul) for the entire resurrected person (body and soul) much like a maritime account of a ship being lost in a storm might refer to the drowning of twenty souls.

That's fine as far as it goes. However, a closer look at Childers' theology reveals more problems concerning the general resurrection. A survey of the book turns up but one reference to the general resurrection and it comes in a large quotation of Tertullian's early third century rule of faith.[206] However, on the very next page Childers cites with approval a scholar named Michael Kruger who summarizes the Patristic rule

---

206 Childers, *Another Gospel?* 90.

of faith while *conspicuously omitting reference to the general resurrection.*[207] Later in the book, Childers approvingly cites Norman Geisler's eight essential doctrines for Christian faith. And once again, the general resurrection is notably absent.[208] So it does seem at the very least that Childers may not value the general resurrection and it may even be the case that she actually denies it.

The fact is, however, that the general resurrection is not only taught in Scripture but has always constituted the very *heart* of Christian eschatological hope and expectation. Let's return again to the statements on the afterlife that we find in the two most universal creeds of the Christian church:

- *Apostles' Creed:* "the resurrection of the body, and the life everlasting."
- *Nicene Creed:* "We look forward to the resurrection of the dead, and to life in the world to come."

Suffice it to say, the general resurrection is *central* to Christian belief, and certainly is far more important than any specific theory of posthumous punishment. With that in mind, there is a rather stark irony that an individual so keen to gauge the orthodoxy of others and name-call them when she sees the slightest superficial similarity to classic heresies like Gnosticism or Marcionism should have such a glaring omission in her own theology.

But is it really a glaring omission in Childers' theology or is it only a glaring omission in this book? To answer that question I turned, finally, to her website and specifically the webpage titled "What I believe."[209] On this page, Childers includes a comprehensive statement of her doctrinal views. Notably, she

---

207 Childers, *Another Gospel?* 91.

208 Childers, *Another Gospel?* 232.

209 https://www.alisachilders.com/what-i-believe.html Accessed March 26, 2022.

includes within the statement her commitment to the eternal punishment of those outside Christ:

> I BELIEVE in the eternal life of the saved and the eternal punishment of the lost.

And once again she omits any reference to belief in the general resurrection. Note that this is the exact opposite of the Apostles' Creed and Nicene Creed which, as we have seen, omit any reference to the nature of posthumous punishment but which both include a ringing endorsement of the general resurrection as their centerpiece.

When I was discussing this omission with someone they replied, "Maybe Childers just didn't get around to mentioning the general resurrection." Didn't get around to it? Keep in mind that her personal statement of faith is *twice as long* as the Apostles' Creed (Childers, "What I Believe,": 234 words; Apostles' Creed in English translation: 115 words). And yet, *she still couldn't be bothered to include in her statement a doctrine at the heart of Christian eschatological hope.* At the same time, she made sure to include a hearty affirmation of the claim that non-Christians suffer forever in hell, a doctrine that is notably *not* included in the ancient creeds. At the very least, it seems to me that her prioritization of doctrine is out of whack with orthodox Christian priorities.

Perhaps the biggest irony is that Childers' theology of the afterlife with its focus on souls and silence on bodies and resurrection looks decidedly . . . gnostic. So while Childers sees fit to judge the orthodoxy of others and accuse them of Gnosticism, it is her own grasp of the orthodox Christian tradition which appears to be tenuous while exhibiting some distinct traits consistent with Gnosticism.

While Childers shows no interest in the central Christian doctrine of the general resurrection, she claims that "progressive Christianity offers me nothing of value. It gives no hope for the afterlife and no joy in this one. It offers a hundred denials with nothing concrete to affirm."[210] On the contrary, several progressive Christians have shown a far more orthodox understanding of the afterlife than Childers with her quasi-gnostic by-passing of the general resurrection. For example, in *The Secret Message of Jesus*, Brian McLaren writes: "For Jesus and for most of his contemporaries, the ultimate hope beyond death was not to live forever in a timeless *disembodied* state away from the earth. Instead, they anticipated resurrection, an embodied state within this creation in a new era or age . . . ."[211] Here, finally, is a robust orthodox affirmation of the great Christian hope, one from which Childers could learn much. Instead, she has the audacity to claim that Christians like McLaren are *without hope*.

Far from lacking hope, McLaren offers a ringing, beautifully orthodox anticipation of our future resurrection, one which is rooted in Jesus Christ, the first fruits of resurrection. He writes: "The unknown frightens us. We want and need comfort and reassurance and hope, especially when facing death. And that is exactly what Jesus offers—and more."[212] "A central element, then, of Jesus' message—and of his life—is this radical confidence that death is not the end, that this life is not all there is, and that there will be a real resurrection."[213] All I can say to that is, Amen! That is a robust and glorious hope indeed, one that is noticeably absent from the hollowness of Childers' truncated confession.

---

210 Childers, *Another Gospel?* 238.

211 McLaren, *The Secret Message of Jesus,* 184.

212 McLaren, *The Secret Message of Jesus,* 185.

213 McLaren, *The Secret Message of Jesus,* 189.

10

Salvation

is Not a List of Beliefs

In the final chapter of *Another Gospel?* Childers turns to the question "What must one affirm in order to be saved?"[214] This is a very important question for Childers to address: given that she claims the foundation of Christianity is doctrine, she needs to be clear on *which doctrines* form that essential foundation of salvation.[215] To answer the question, Childers ultimately defers to the conclusions of conservative evangelical theologian Norman Geisler. She writes:

Geisler concluded that, according to the New Testament, the essentials one must believe (at least implicitly) in order to be saved today are

1.Human depravity (I am a sinner);
2.God's unity (There is one God);

214 Childers, *Another Gospel?* 232.

215 I critique that notion of salvation in terms of doctrinal assent at some length in *What's So Confusing About Grace?*

3.The necessity of grace (I am saved by grace);

4.Christ's deity (Christ is God);

5.Christ's humanity (Christ is man);

6.Christ's atoning death (Christ died for my sins)

7.Christ's bodily resurrection (Christ rose from the dead); and

8.The necessity of faith (I must believe).

So for people to call themselves Christians, they must at least implicitly believe these eight things. [216]

To be honest, this passage raises many more questions than it answers.[217] For starters, the list doesn't even *mention* core Christian doctrines like the Trinity even though this doctrine has been justly called *the cornerstone* of all Christian doctrine. I would think that is a rather significant oversight, no?

Geisler's list also doesn't include the general resurrection. As we saw in the last chapter, Childers likewise neglects to affirm this doctrine either in her book or in the "What I believe" section on her website, this despite the fact that the general resurrection is prominent in both the Apostles' and Nicene Creeds and has always been the centerpiece of Christian eschatological hope tied into Christ as the firstfruits for our future resurrection (1 Corinthians 15:20).

How could Geisler and Childers possibly think that believing that one must believe (doctrine 8) is more essential than core confessions like the Trinity and general resurrection?

When it comes to eschatology, the general resurrection isn't the only doctrine that is missing. Geisler's list includes nothing else about eternity, no mention of the new heavens and new earth, eternal life, or judgment. On the upside, at least

---

216 Childers, *Another Gospel?* 232-3.

217 I have not read Geisler's book, so I cannot comment directly on the extent to which he may address any of my questions or critiques. Thus, my specific target is Geisler's position *as it is quoted and represented by Childers.*

he doesn't include eternal conscious torment in his shortlist of essentials, so that's a bit of a silver lining, I suppose.

There are several other general problems with attempts to tie salvation essentially to a list of beliefs. The binary mind-set wants to think of belief as either something you have or something you don't, but as we have seen the reality is far more complex. Belief can wax and wane over time, sometimes moving for periods into the shadow space of agnostic uncertainty or unbelief and then back again. So if Geisler is going to insist that we must believe these doctrines in order to be saved by Christ, he certainly owes us some kind of account of *how strongly* and *how frequently* one must confess them. Remember Childers' derision toward a pastor who would admit to being (on occasion) only 60 percent sure? Her criticism would suggest that that degree of conviction isn't enough to be saved. In that case, how much conviction *is* required? And if your belief drops below that threshold in a dark night of doubt, are you lost for that night?

Implicit Belief from Blastocysts to Buddhists

All of these are merely initial critical responses to a list of "essential beliefs for salvation" that, as I said, raises far more questions than it answers. For the remainder of this chapter, I want to focus in on some of the problems with this view vis-à-vis the very wooly notion of implicit belief. You see, one of the biggest puzzles is the qualification that one must believe these doctrines "at least *implicitly.*" What does that look like? When do you know if a person has implicit belief? Let's focus in on that specific question with some detailed scenarios.

The Blastocyst. Let's assume that life begins at conception.[218] Approximately five days after conception, the early developing human being is a blastocyst, a tiny structure (approximately 1.5

---

218 It's a safe bet that Childers would agree given her comments on abortion. See *Another Gospel?* 76, 163.

mm across) consisting of between 200 to 300 cells. Do human beings who die at the blastocyst stage go to hell? Or do they all implicitly believe 1-8? If the former, how could God send a human being to hell to be tortured forever because they died at the blastocyst stage when they never even had an opportunity to believe 1-8? If the latter, what would it even *mean* to say a hollow ball of 250 cells implicitly believes this list of doctrines?

Like I said, I have questions, so many questions.

Hannah. Next, consider the case of a twelve-year-old Jewish girl at Auschwitz named Hannah. On the night before she is to be killed in the gas chamber, a sympathetic Lutheran Nazi guard whispers to her that she must accept that Jesus is Lord in order to be saved. She whispers back to him angrily, "I want nothing to do with your Jesus." I would think that's an understandable response given the present circumstances. After all, would you be inclined to accept a savior whom you took to be in league with the genocidaires currently killing all your family, friends, and acquaintances?

And so, unlike the blastocyst, it seems that Hannah professes actively to *disbelieve* in Jesus. Does that mean that she is going from the gas chamber to a resurrection into hell where she will be tortured forever? Or might Geisler and Childers come up with an interesting way that Hannah "implicitly" believes 1-8 despite her avowed rejection of Jesus?

The kindhearted Buddhist. In her chapter on hell, Childers addresses the awkward topic of a "kindhearted Buddhist who bathed and fed the homeless".[219] According to Childers' calculus, he is clearly in hell irrespective of his life of love and service because he failed to believe Geiser's eight doctrines. Lest you think it is unfair that this kindhearted Buddhist will be in anguish forever, Childers adds that at least he will probably not be tortured with the same degree of intensity as Adolf Hitler. I'm not kidding, she actually says that: "So what about the kindhearted Buddhist who bathed and fed the homeless?

---

219 Childers, *Another Gospel?* 194.

If he dies before he puts his faith in Christ, will he get the same punishment as Hitler . . . ? I don't think so."[220] Childers goes on to explain that there are levels of punishment: the worse the sin, the more intense the punishment. Since Hitler was bombing cities and gassing Jews while the Buddhist was er, binding wounds, Hitler will be tortured with greater intensity than the Buddhist. Though rest assured both will still be tortured eternally.

Um, okay, that's a sort of concession, I guess.

Jesus Broadens the Horizon

Once again, Childers repeats the same error she made with atonement and hell of assuming Christians are obliged to accept her interpretation of a doctrine not only as a requirement of orthodoxy but even of salvation. In this case, we are obliged to *believe that one must believe* if we are to be saved (Geisler's point 8) and what one must believe includes doctrines 1-7.

There is just so much wrong here that it is hard to know where to begin: the mind-numbing implausibility of insisting that every human blastocyst that dies either believed 1-8 "implicitly" or they will be subject to an eternity of torture in hell; the prospect that a 12-year-old Jewish girl murdered by "Christians" who denied Geisler's list goes from the temporal gas chamber to the eternal torture chamber; the notion that torturing a "kindhearted Buddhist" for eternity is more palatable if he is tortured with less intensity than Adolf Hitler. This truly is a catalogue of impossible things to believe before breakfast.

Thank goodness that despite Childers' insistence to the contrary, her narrow sectarianism that rests Christianity on her chosen set of doctrines and damns everyone else is not the only game in town. In 2013, Pope Francis offered a homily on Mark 9:38-40:

---

220 Childers, *Another Gospel?* 197.

"Teacher," said John, "we saw someone driving out demons in your name and we told him to stop, because he was not one of us."

"Do not stop him," Jesus said. "For no one who does a miracle in my name can in the next moment say anything bad about me, for whoever is not against us is for us."

In preaching on the passage, Pope Francis observed that the apostles responded indignantly toward the outsiders, thinking that they alone possessed the truth of God:

> They complain. "If he is not one of us, he cannot do good. If he is not of our party, he cannot do good." And Jesus corrects them: "Do not hinder him" he says, "let him do good" . . . . They were a little intolerant . . . those who do not have the truth, cannot do good. This was wrong . . . Jesus broadens the horizon. The root of this possibility of doing good—that we all have—is in creation.
>
> The Lord created us in His image and likeness, and we are the image of the Lord, and He does good and all of us have this commandment at heart: do good and do not do evil. All of us. "But Father, this is not Catholic! He cannot do good." Yes he can . . . . 'The Lord has redeemed all of us, all of us, with the Blood of Christ: all of us, not just Catholics. Everyone! "Father, the atheists?" Even the atheists. Everyone! . . . We must meet one another doing good.[221]

I don't need to tell you that Pope Francis' homily is a direct rebuttal to Geisler's doctrine 8 "The necessity of faith (I must believe)." Given that Geisler insists that assent to doctrine 8 is required for salvation, it seems to follow that Pope Francis is going to hell where he will be tortured forever. I'm not the biggest fan of the papacy, but eternal torture seems a bit much.

---

221 Cited in Don Erickson, *A Life Lived and Laid Down for Friends: A Progressive Christology* (Resource, 2019), 106-7.

I don't buy that. Pope Francis is merely one example (though a particularly significant one!) in a long line of Christians who have rejected Geisler's doctrine 8. Indeed, that alternative theology, which is known as inclusivism, has been the standard position of the Catholic Church since Vatican II. And it has been defended by Christians from apologist Justin Martyr in the second century to leading evangelicals like John Sanders in our own day.[222]

In the following passage, the sixteenth century Protestant Reformer Ulrich Zwingli lists some of the people he believes will be found in God's Kingdom who are from outside the Judeo-Christian trajectory of revelation. His list includes "Hercules too and Theseus, Socrates, Aristides, Antigonus, Numa, Camillus, the Catos and Scipios . . . ." In other words, Zwingli gives us a who's who of admired Greek and Roman pagan philosophers, poets, and even demigods (Hercules!) who will be included in God's kingdom alongside confessing Christians and pious Jews. Zwingli then expands his point: "In short there has not lived a single good man, there has not been a single pious heart or believing soul from the beginning of the world to the end, which you will not see there in the presence of God. Can we conceive of any spectacle more joyful or agreeable or indeed sublime?"[223]

Presumably, Childers would not find the spectacle of pagans being saved to be joyful or agreeable, let alone sublime. But then why should the salvation of Theseus or Socrates be any more surprising than the salvation of [insert your name here]? As Pope Francis said, Jesus broadens the horizon. While Childers is quick to damn anyone who doesn't endorse her sectarian theology, Jesus instead invites us to find out where he is working

---

222 See John Sanders, *No Other Name: An Investigation into the Destiny of the Unevangelized* (Eerdmans, 1992).

223 Cited in William Stacy Johnson and John H. Leith, *Reformed Reader: A Sourcebook in Christian Theology*, vol. 1, *Classical Beginnings: 1519-1799* (Westminster John Knox, 1993), 386-7.

in the world beyond the walls of our pet theology. And if there is one lesson to be taken from the Gospels, it is that the space where Jesus works is often far outside the sphere of his confessing followers. Remember his long list of friends included tax collectors and Canaanites, women caught in adultery and prostitutes, lepers, the poor, downtrodden, and forgotten.

Constrained by their narrow sectarian paradigm, conservative evangelicals like Childers simply don't have a framework to process the expansive work of Christ and his Spirit. In their view, their doctrinal confession (Geisler's 1-8) provides the necessary delimiting factor in all God's work. And so, they tend to dismiss a hopeful expanding of the horizons with such reactionary and ham-fisted labels as "pluralism" or "works righteousness." But it is none of those things. Rather, it is simply a recognition of the words of Jesus that "whoever is not against us is for us." If you really want a read on where the Kingdom of God is advancing, you should begin not with those who profess Geisler's shortlist of essential doctrines, but rather with those who truly live out the love of neighbor.

Two Gospels: A Final Word

On page 91, Childers cites Michael Kruger's summary of the Gospel in seven propositions including God as creator, Jesus' incarnating into the world to bring salvation and the fact that he is resurrected and coming again. She then quotes the following statement from Brian McLaren:

> [Jesus] came to announce a new kingdom, a new way of life, a new way of peace that carried good news to all people of every religion. A new kingdom is much bigger than a new religion, and in fact it has room for many religious traditions within it. This good news wasn't simply about a new way to solve the religious problems of ontological fall and original sin (problems, remember once more, that arise centuries later

and within a different narrative altogether). It wasn't simply information about how individual souls could leave earth, avoid hell, and ascend to heaven after death. No, it was about God's will being done on earth as in heaven for all people. It was about God's faithful solidarity with all humanity in our suffering, oppression, and evil. It was about God's compassion and call to be reconciled with God and with one another—before death on earth.[224]

I think that's a wonderful statement! Of course, Alisa Childers disagrees: "These two gospels" she says, "couldn't be more different."[225]

Childers' opinion notwithstanding, the truth is that Brian McLaren has a far more robust and *orthodox* understanding of the Gospel than her narrow sectarian evangelicalism. McLaren eloquently recognizes that Jesus broke down simple in-group/ out-group distinctions with expanded horizons that invite us to see his Kingdom emerging in endless ways beyond our narrow religious communities; the Augustinian account of sin and the fall is but one story that has been told in the Christian tradition and, as with theories like penal substitutionary atonement or eternal conscious torment, it has never been a required doctrine of orthodox Christian confession; salvation isn't just about souls avoiding hell but about the redemption of creation as reflected in the hope of a new heaven and new earth.

If Childers think this description "couldn't be more different" than the Christian Gospel, then perhaps she doesn't really understand that Gospel in the first place. Needless to say, you should always have a thorough understanding of the Gospel before you proceed to accuse others of having abandoned it.

---

224 Childers, *Another Gospel?* 92.

225 Childers, *Another Gospel?* 92.

Epilogue

A Request
and an Invitation

Dear Alisa Childers,
I did not enjoy writing this book, but I was compelled to do so because you are slandering fellow Christians and leading your readers astray into the errors of your conservative evangelical theology. I am not claiming you intended to do this. It could be that you are simply not aware that the doctrines which you believe to be mere Christianity are, in fact, the product of your take on conservative North American Protestantism. Regardless, by insisting that others accept your narrow understanding of doctrines like atonement, hell, and the role of confession in salvation, you "tie up heavy, cumbersome loads and put them on other people's shoulders." (Matthew 23:4) Further, you testify falsely about fellow Christians who disagree with you by denying that they are Christians at all. You marginalize their voices with false and toxic labels like gnostic and Marcionite. You adopt incendiary and dehumanizing rhetoric by claiming they are evil wolves who only want to take a bite out of hapless sheep.

That is hurtful and false. These people you attack by name are not wolves, Alisa Childers. They are fellow Christians, disciples on the way just like you. They are saved by the same savior that you profess, and they care about the truth every bit as much as you do. And they don't want to lead others astray any more than you do. Granted, they are not perfect, and no doubt, they make their share of theological errors. Just like we all do. Just like *you* do. But they do *not* preach another gospel. On the contrary, they preach the faith once for all delivered unto the saints. They do not serve a different Lord but rather the one incarnate Lord at the heart of Christian faith. The truth is that at multiple points, their theology is far more generous, nuanced, and *orthodox* than the narrow sectarianism you have confused with mere Christianity. Ms. Childers, I don't doubt that you love Jesus. But you need to understand that the boundaries of those who love Jesus extend far beyond your sectarian confession. So please stop slandering your fellow Christians and spreading falsehoods about them.

Now I want to conclude by addressing the reader who may have found yourself resonating with the discussion in this book and desiring to hear more. The good news is that there is a live, vibrant conversation that is ongoing right now. It involves millions of Christians around the world who share a desire to think through their faith in honesty and rigor and without fear of censure. They are your brothers and sisters in Christ and they welcome different opinions. They are not afraid to wrestle as Jacob wrestled with the angel. And they have saved a place at the table for you.

Also Available from 2 Cup Press

Jesus Loves Canaanites

In this bold new book, Randal Rauser defends a novel approach to the Canaanite genocide, one that remains faithful to our deepest moral intuitions even as it is guided by the conviction that Jesus calls us to love all our neighbors.

....

Available for purchase (print and e-book) at major online retailers including Amazon and Barnes & Noble.

2 CUP
PRESS

Made in the USA
Las Vegas, NV
08 August 2022